Torres Strait

Great

Barrier

Reef

Hinchinbrook I.

Whitsunday Group

EENSLAND

New Caledonia

Fraser I.

BRISBANE

NEW SOUTH WALES

Norfolk I.

Lord Howe I.

SYDNEY

CTORIA

MELBOURNE

Some of the Countless

hillip I.

I. ৬

Bass Strait

Islands

Launceston

ANIA

HOBART

NEXT DOOR TO PARADISE
Australia's Countless Islands

5/11

Next Door to Paradise

Australia's Countless Islands

BILL BEATTY

CASSELL AUSTRALIA

CASSELL AUSTRALIA LTD
210 Queen Street, Melbourne, Victoria
AND AT
SYDNEY · LONDON · TORONTO · CAPETOWN
JOHANNESBURG · AUCKLAND

Registered at the General Post Office, Melbourne,
for transmission by post as a book

Printed and bound in Australia by Wilke and Company Limited,
19-47 Jeffcott Street, Melbourne

F.964

Contents

List of Illustrations

The author and publishers wish to thank the following for their
helpful assistance in the compiling of the illustrations in this
book:

Australian News and Information Service; The West Australian
Department of Information; The Queensland Government Tour-
ist Bureau; The South Australian Tourist Bureau; The Tourist
Development Association of Victoria; The New South Wales
Department of Tourist Activities and Immigration. Also 'Walka-
bout' magazine and Douglass Baglin Photography Ltd.

Foreword

ISLAND living has a primitive appeal to all of us. Every man, sooner or later, feels the irresistible call of the islands stirring his blood — the strangely fascinating remoteness of island life. How often we weary of civilization and have the urge to get away from it all and live a back-to-nature life. Fishing, the tang of the sea, lying on a lonely beach watching the lazy breakers curling on the white sands or swimming in the quiet waters of a palm fringed lagoon — these things fuse themselves into the spell of our island dreams.

Australia is immensely rich in islands, from the island State of Tasmania to the innumerable islets of the Coral Sea. Although the 'Apple Isle' is not included in this survey (Tasmania was the subject of my previous book) all the main islands are covered as well as many little-known ones.

The Whitsunday Group alone comprises 106 islands; Lord Howe is not one but a group of 28 islands and islets on some of which no man has set foot. No one has counted the thousands of islands, islets and coral cays of the Great Barrier Reef — the task would be an impossible one. Bass Strait, the Gulf of Carpentaria, the coast of Arnhem Land have many islands, all with their individual characteristics and attractions.

For all its vastness Australia itself is still an island — and until recent times was held to the rest of the world only by ships. And just as this island-continent is a land of contrast with her great beaches, tremendous snowfields, tropical North and yawning Outback, so her countless islands reveal striking individuality from the charming old-world atmosphere pervading Quality Row in Kingston, the 'capital' of Norfolk

Island, to the chromium-plated luxury of some of the tourist resorts and the lonesome Robinson Crusoe-like islands of the far North. Moreover, a wealth of dramatic stories — tales of high adventure, shipwreck, tragedy and romance — surround very many of these islands, for they have seen Australia in the making.

From the time of my first visit as a youth to Daydream, a coral island off the Great Barrier Reef, to a sojourn on the Arnhem Land islands of Bathurst and Melville in 1964, I have been intrigued by this country's heritage of islands. Some of them, because of their isolation and lack of transport facilities, cannot be visited under ordinary circumstances. Also, a special permit is necessary to visit a few of the missionary islands. Nevertheless, even such off-the-beaten track groups as the Abrolhos of Western Australia are now included in tourist trips from the mainland, and a regular fortnightly air service operates from Darwin to islands (hopping from one to another) right around to the Gulf of Carpentaria. What were once little known and seldom visited island outposts of Australia are today comparatively easy of access.

In a world of strain and anxiety, life in these arcadian regions remains peaceful and serene. Here time stands still. Here, so close to the Australian coastline yet seemingly thousands of miles away, is this island paradise where Nature's creative power is displayed in so much that is rich and beautiful to delight the eye and the contemplative mind.

BILL BEATTY.

I

The Island of Mist

'HERE it seems that nature has spared nothing to render this isle delightful above all others that I have ever seen . . .' So wrote the Dutch navigator, Willem de Vlamingh, when he visited Rottnest Island in 1696. He then went on to describe the island as 'a terrestrial paradise', which he named 'Rottnest' because, as he records in his log, of the presence of a little animal which he thought to be some species of rat; the word Rottnest meaning Rats' Nest. We now know that this friendly little marsupial, which is the island's pride, is the quokka — a unique member of the wallaby family.

De Vlamingh is remembered with the historic Vlamingh Plate, an inscribed piece of pewter, circular in shape and approximately 14 inches in diameter, which ranks, next to the Hartog Plate, as the oldest known relic of European contact with Australia. Dating from 1697, it is Dutch in origin but, after remaining on Dirk Hartog Island off the Western Australian coast for many years, it was possessed by a museum in France for more than a century, after which it was returned to Australia. Following a period of display in the National Library, Canberra, the plate was presented by the Commonwealth Government to Western Australia, and it is now in possession of the trustees of the Museum and Art Gallery of Perth.

Rottnest Island has been called the Island of Mist because of its remarkable mirages which, seen from the sea, give an illusion of the island being suspended and reflected in mid-air. This phenomenon was also noted by Vlamingh. He was not the discoverer of the island; thirty-eight years before his

1

visit members of the crew of another Dutch expedition under Samuel Volkerson landed on Rottnest, but the records of it are meagre.

Today, Rottnest is the premier island resort in Western Australia. It is only eleven miles north-west from Fremantle and is well-serviced by steamer. An air service also operates to Rottnest, which holds the distinction of being the world's shortest regular air route. The island measures approximately seven miles in length by three miles at the widest point, and has an area of 4,726 acres. Rottnest has considerable natural beauty, the coastline being indented with numerous bays throughout, and jutting headlands, whose rocky buttresses have been fretted by the action of the sea into fantastic caves and grottos, shell-strewn beaches; wooded forelands delight and fascinate the eye. A succession of extensive and very beautiful salt lakes of ultramarine blue contrast enchantingly with the vivid green of the wooded slopes.

At one time the island was a pilot station for the Port of Fremantle; later it was used also as an internment camp. During World War II, because of its strategic position, Rottnest was taken over as a military establishment. It is governed by a Board of Control which is responsible to the Western Australian Government. Its main lighthouse is the first Australian landmark for incoming ships.

No matter what impressions are engendered by a visit to Rottnest, one is always conscious of a feeling for its history, and you begin to realize that the history of this little island holds much of its charm. The aborigines of the mainland knew it by the name of Wadjemup, but there is no evidence that any aborigines lived on it at any time or even visited it. The Rottnest story begins in 1658, with the visit of Volkerson, followed later by Vlamingh, who is commemorated by a memorial erected on View Hill, overlooking a sweeping panorama of the island.

Rottnest was a convict settlement for some ten years and its main buildings are those erected by the prisoners. Though of rough stone and rather primitive design they nevertheless retain a certain charm associated with early colony days. At a later date a vice-regal residence was built and a number of

Western Australia's early administrators made it their summer home. A large area of land adjacent to Government House was out of bounds to the other inhabitants of the island, and the vice-regal parties spent much of their leisure in shooting and fishing.

The most conspicuous of the native trees is the Rottnest Pine, which bears a resemblance to the Cedar of Lebanon. The Tea (or Ti) Tree abounds there as does also the Climbing Clematis. The Rottnest Daisy although found on the mainland, is regarded as something typical of the island. It grows prolifically, and during the months of November and December hills and valleys are covered by a profusion of its delicate, lavender-coloured blossoms. Earlier in the year vivid splashes of colour from the scarlet Templetonia shrubs enhance the island's landscape.

Visitors take great interest in the quokka, the little animal which is a characteristic feature of Rottnest. Quokka is the aboriginal name for this miniature scrub-wallaby. There was a time when quokkas were very common in the South-West of Western Australia, but they no longer exist on the Australian mainland. Apart from Rottnest, their only other habitat is Bald Head, off Albany in the far south. The quokka usually moves along on all fours and sometimes it climbs several feet up into the foliage of thickets, apparently to feed on shoots.

The zoology department of the University of Western Australia started an investigation into the habits of the quokka some years ago. In 1954 the Commonwealth Scientific and Industrial Research Organization wild life survey section became interested in the animal, particularly in the need for a population study. The aim of investigations at Rottnest at present is to find the best method of censusing the quokka, so that changes in its population can be followed. As many quokkas as possible are caught and marked with an ear tag, to which is attached reflecting tape, or a plastic collar, with reflecting tape patterns.

The work has two main aspects. One is to measure the population and study changes in it with a view to better conservation of rare species. The other is to obtain better control of the species. Today there are about 10,000 of these mites on the island, tame enough to take morsels from tourists' hands. More than 2,200 quokkas have been marked and many have been recaptured several times, giving valuable information on movements, behaviour, growth and survival.

The island abounds in bird life. More than 130 varieties have been recorded by ornithologists — everything from peacock to mutton-bird. Wild duck and snipe abound in the vicinity of the lakes on Rottnest. These salt lakes spread over a large area of the island; limpid and calm they mirror the light and brilliance of the sky and reflect the trees along their banks. The salt content of the lakes is high (a favourite trick for the tourist is to sit in one of the lakes reading a paper. It's impossible to sink.) and the picturesque old saltworks is another reminder of bygone days when the collection and processing of salt was the island's first industry.

A wonderful panorama opens before the visitor who mounts the 130-foot tower of the main lighthouse — to the west the breakers of Cape Vlamingh, to the south Garden and Carnac Islands, to the east the grey outline of the mainland coast, to the north the old convict settlement. Garden Island, visible from the tower, is often visited during the summer by tourists, but there is no settlement on the island.

The reef-strewn coast of Rottnest is identified with the wrecks of many sailing-vessels, for, with the hazy charts of those times, the passage to the port of Fremantle was a hazardous one. Underwater photographers and explorers delight in delving among these wrecks. There are at least ten of these ill-fated vessels: the *Lancer* (1839), the *Transit* (1842), the *Gem* (1876), *Lady Elizabeth* (1878), *Macedon* (1883), *Mira Flores* (1886), *Janet* (1887), *Denton Holme* (1890), *Raven* (1891), *City of York* (1899).

The waters off Rottnest are also the graveyard for a fleet of five famous Catalina aircraft which Qantas used in the epic Indian Ocean crossings during World War II. As the aircraft were given to Australia by the United States through Lend-Lease they could not be made available for civil or

4

other peacetime purposes, so there was no alternative when the war ended but to destroy them. They were subsequently sunk off Rottnest in the Indian Ocean which they had so proudly conquered.

Rottnest Island has had its share of drama and romance. Legend tells of a duel that was fought by members of the crew of a French ship under the command of Commodore Nicholas Baudin while it was in Western Australian waters in the year 1803. The duel was fought over a girl whom both men had loved in France. One man was killed and buried on the island. The victor is said to have returned to Rottnest some thirty or forty years later as the skipper of a merchant ship. Instinct took him to the burial place of his rival; and before leaving the island he left money with one of the residents so that a tombstone could be erected on the grave. To this day in the little Rottnest graveyard the tombstone still remains, but any inscription on it has long since become obliterated.

Rottnest was the scene, too, of the dramatic escape of the Irish political prisoner John Boyle O'Reilly. Nearly one hundred years have passed since O'Reilly absconded from the island and went to America, but every year a wreath-laying party formed of members of the Boston 'Catalpa Society' salutes his statue in their city. It was from Boston that O'Reilly helped organize the escape of six more Irishmen from these shores in the U.S. whaler *Catalpa*.

Imperial Convict No. 9,843, John Boyle O'Reilly, arrived at Fremantle Port on January 10, 1868, by the prison-ship *Hougomont*. He was described in the gaol records as 'of healthy appearance, aged 25 years, 5 ft. 7 ½ins. in height, black hair, brown eyes, oval visage, dark complexion: an Irishman'. The charm of O'Reilly's personality can be gauged from his treatment on the transport *Hougomont* that brought him to Australia. Instead of being herded below deck with other political prisoners and the criminals, he was well treated by the ship's officers in the night watches. He was allowed to use the captain's library and he edited a shipboard weekly paper called 'The Wild Goose'.

Son of a National teacher, he was born at Dowth Castle, near Drogheda, and became a reporter on a Preston newspaper in England. He enlisted in the Lancashire Volunteers and developed Fenian sympathies. This led to his joining the 10th Hussars in Ireland where, like many of his comrades, he wore the red coat of Britain on his back, but the green flag of Erin in his heart. In February, 1866, he was charged with 'knowing the preparations for a mutiny and not informing his superior officer'. And so he arrived in Australia under a sentence of twenty years imprisonment.

O'Reilly confided to a visiting priest, Father McCabe, that he intended absconding but the priest warned him not to try a hopeless break for the bush but to bide his time and he might be able to help him. Months later a friend of Father McCabe approached O'Reilly, who was working in a road gang, and told him that the skipper of an American whaler was due to visit the port and was willing to pick him up if he could contrive to get outside the three-mile limit to sea.

Breaking camp shortly afterwards, O'Reilly walked three miles to a rendezvous with the friend of the priest who had brought horses. They rode to the beach and took a boat to Rottnest Island where an English settler was waiting to supply them with a meal. He informed O'Reilly that a ticket-of-leave man named Martin Bowman, a convicted thug and one of the worst characters in the colony had heard of the escape plan and insisted on being taken along as a price of silence. There was nothing else for it and he was taken aboard the whaler.

Two months later the whaler *Gazelle* dropped anchor at Port Mathurin in the British island of Rodriguez. The Governor came aboard announcing that he was looking for two desperate escaped convicts from Western Australia, named O'Reilly and Bowman. He requested a ship's muster. From the descriptions, Bowman was recognized and arrested, but O'Reilly passed the muster without recognition. It was a certainty that Bowman would inform on his fellow-escapee in the hope of mitigating his own punishment.

In the deepening dusk that evening there was a sudden splash and the cry 'Man overboard!' But although many

6

Rottnest Island, Western Australia

Islands in the Torres Strait

Original colonial quarters, Rottnest Island

sharp eyes scanned the waters of the island all that could be found and retrieved from the grey-green swell was the hat of John Boyle O'Reilly. 'The Wild Goose' had, alas, flown west! 'Poor fellow!' said the skipper, 'he swore that he would never be taken alive!'

In the morning the ship's flag was flying at half-mast when the Governor with a strong escort came aboard the *Gazelle* again, bringing the informer Bowman to identify O'Reilly. Sadly the captain told the Governor of O'Reilly's suicide. The Governor said he would have divers search for the body but decided against it when he remembered that the sharks would make short work of any body in those waters. Besides, the Governor's wife was Irish . . .

The death of O'Reilly was entered in the island's records, and the *Gazelle* raised her anchor. Once on the high seas, the mate opened a locker on the deck and released the 'drowned' Fenian, who was joyfully reunited with the crew and sailed by devious routes to America. There he won fame as writer and poet, dying 20 years later, a revered editor of the 'Boston Pilot', aged 46. Many years after his rescue he wrote a novel entitled *'Moondyne; an Australian Story'*. This is one of the little-known treasures of Australian literature; O'Reilly's gifted pen reveals a vivid memory of this country with a respect for the aborigines and a deep appreciation of the bush second only to his love of the Emerald Isle.

With no private vehicles permitted on Rottnest Island there is little to disturb the tranquillity. Few can visit Rottnest without coming under the subtle spell which the island exerts and which reaches from the past. You feel that there you are truly in another world; a world redolent of sweet-smelling trees and herbage, the salty tang of the sea, and the atmosphere of bygone days. In the eagerness of those who come again and again to Rottnest, and in the reluctance of those departing, it is easy to discern a real affection for the island.

2

Islands of History

OF Western Australia's uninhabited islands none is more historical than the Houtman Abrolhos group or the Monte Bello Islands. The former, sometimes called the Houtman Rocks, or the Abrolhos Islands, comprises three groups — Wallaby, Easter and Pelsart — and coral-islet outriders which lie in the Indian Ocean about 45 miles west of Geraldton, and which extend about 50 miles in a north-westerly direction. The name repeats that of a dangerous group of reefs, much dreaded by sailors, off the coast of Brazil.

The Abrolhos, although entirely composed of coral or part coral, are unlike the islands of the Barrier Reef region. The Wallaby Islands form the largest and most interesting subgroup of the Abrolhos. Part of the surface of these islands is sand which is burrowed everywhere by the mutton-birds, the same species as that which nests on Heron Island and other islets off the Queensland coast. There was a time when much of the surface of the Abrolhos groups was covered with a rich deposit of guano, but most of it was removed and sold during the early years of this century. During World War II the islands were a source of phosphate supplies. The existence of the guano is proof of the notable part the Abrolhos have played as the nesting places of sea birds.

The Wallaby Islands are remarkable for the presence of large numbers of wallabies and other mainland animals. How they came to make their homes on low coral isles far out to sea is a mystery. Certainly no one conveyed the animals there, but perhaps these islands have an ancient connection with the mainland of Western Australia.

The Easter Group is about fourteen miles south of the Wallaby Islands and a narrow channel separates the former from the Pelsart Group, which is the best known of all. Although the Abrolhos cannot be described as beautiful — their plant life is mostly mangroves and dull-coloured shrubs — the Pelsart Group has magnificent coral growths in its lagoons of which there is nothing finer on the Great Barrier Reef. The bird life of these islands is extraordinary. One ornithologist has recorded that the Abrolhos 'form the greatest rookery for sea birds in Australia and by reason of their geographical position in the sub-tropics, perhaps afford suitable breeding grounds for a greater number of species than any other distinct or limited spot in the world'.

The Geraldton Tourist Bureau organizes trips to the Abrolhos, the main attraction being the fishing grounds. The waters of these isles are a fisherman's paradise; no less than two million pounds of lobsters alone have been caught there in one year.

A grim yet fascinating background of murder, mutiny, piracy and treasure, hangs like a sombre mantle over the Abrolhos, their discoverer having been that Frederick Houtman, who, in the early seventeenth century, was engaged by the Dutch East India Company to command a fleet of eleven ships sent from Holland to the far distant Spice Islands, there to negotiate and load for the home market those exotic products which made the East Indies trade so profitable.

The route of the voyage from Amsterdam to Batavia was via the Cape of Good Hope, the east coast of Africa, and across the Indian Ocean — a journey that usually took twelve months. When Houtman and his fleet of vessels set out on the expedition in 1617 he travelled further eastward than he intended and made a landfall on the Western Australian coast where the town of Geraldton now stands. In his journals he described the land as 'a level, broken country with reefs all around it'. He marked the position of certain islands on his map, and named them the Abrolhos, a Portuguese word meaning 'Look out!'. The name was prophetic.

Eleven years later, Francis Pelsart was given command of

the ship *Batavia* by a group of Amsterdam merchants. The *Batavia* was commissioned to engage in the South Seas trade. She carried a fortune in silver and a wealth of valuable merchandise for trading purposes. She also carried a very mixed company. It included adventurous spirits, both men and women, who were going to Batavia and elsewhere to make their fortunes, and who were not over-particular as to the methods they might adopt to gain their ends. The crew was drawn from the scum of the Amsterdam waterfront, and even the officers were not the strongest team that could have been selected.

Trouble was inevitable; it broke out early in the voyage when it became plain that the captain — next in rank to Pelsart — was neglecting his navigation for the women on board. Half the crew put their heads together and planned to take the ship by surprise, throw overboard those who wouldn't join them, and turn pirates. But before this dashing exploit could be carried out, the coast of Western Australia was sighted, and shortly afterwards the ship ran aground on one of the islands of the Abrolhos.

Passengers and crew now found themselves in a hopeless situation on the reefs. They salvaged provisions and chests of money and jewels. It is known that four chests of scarlet, cloth of gold and silver fabrics, and three boxes of silver and antiques were salvaged and stored somewhere on the reefs. A few hundred gallons of water were saved but this would not last long with more than two hundred people. There was no water on any of the islands, and unless it rained it was plain that they would perish. The commander, Pelsart, with the captain and a few officers made a search for water on the mainland of the Western Australian coast but could find none. Pelsart then decided to make the dangerous voyage to Batavia in a small open boat to seek help.

When weeks passed and Pelsart failed to return, one of the ship's officers — Cornelius — assumed command with the idea of building a smaller vessel from the timbers of the wreck, and, with a few kindred souls sailing away on a career of piracy. The rest of the castaways, it was decided, would be killed. About fifty cut-throats were selected as

Cornelius's comrades in crime, and an attractive woman was ear-marked for each. This important business completed, it was decided that the rest of the ship's company and passengers must be disposed of.

The following night about one hundred men and women were massacred. Stabbed or beaten to death, their bodies were thrown into the sea. In celebration of their victory the murderers opened kegs of wine and decked themselves out in rich embroidered velvets and costly silks that had been brought out on the ill-fated vessel for the merchants of Batavia.

But even the most perfectly conceived plans sometimes come unstuck; during the slaughter, a few of the attacked party escaped to one of the adjacent islands. When the would-be pirates got over their drunken orgy they attempted to land on the island where the litle band had taken refuge, but the fugitives beat them back each time.

In the meantime Pelsart had reached Batavia, obtained help, and returned to the scene of the shipwreck on board the frigate *Sardam*. A bloody hand-to-hand fight ensued in which all the mutineers were captured. Pelsart had the ringleaders hanged on the spot, after erecting the gallows with his own hands. The rest were taken to Batavia to be dealt with in more conventional fashion.

Before leaving, a start was made to transfer to the *Sardam* the silver aboard the *Batavia*. (The latter vessel did not sink; she remained perched on the treacherous ridge which had broken her back.) A sudden storm sprang up and the *Batavia* broke in two and sank below the waves. To this day no one has succeeded in raising the treasure.

The wreck of the *Batavia* provided the first written record of the wallaby. Pelsart was also the first man to record a land-bird in Australia; he saw 'a number of grey turtle-doves' — probably bronzewing pigeons — on one of the islands.

Among other ships that later were wrecked on the Abrolhos was the Dutch ship *Zeewyk* in 1727. Members of her crew landed on Gun Island and from the ship's timbers constructed a small sloop which they called the *Slopie* and sailed to Batavia. The Abrolhos were thus the first place in Australian territory where white men built a ship. The wreck of the *Ocean Queen* on Pelsart Island in 1840 provided an opportunity for the noted naturalist and explorer, John Gilbert, to visit the area; he joined a salvage party sent to the wreck and recorded the great gatherings of sea-birds that frequent the islands in the nesting-season.

The group of islets and rocky outcrops known as the Monte Bello Islands lies off the north-west coast of Western Australia, approximately fifty miles north-west of Cape Preston. Part of an extensive coral reef, the main islands of the group are North West, Trimouille, South East, and Hermite. About ten miles to the south of the group lies the much larger Barrow Island.

The Monte Bello Islands are of coral and limestone formation, covered with sand and spinifex, and the sheltered bays are edged with mangroves. Wild cats and wallabies together with a number of species of birds inhabit the islands, and green turtle and fish are plentiful. The islands were the scene of the first atomic explosion carried out by the British Government; this took place on October 3, 1952, under the supervision of a joint party of Australian and British experts.

The Monte Bello group was also the scene of Australia's first recorded shipwreck. The luckless vessel — the *Trial* — was also the first English ship to sight the then unknown fifth continent. Probably there were many wrecks before the year 1622 on the unnamed Australian coast, but the letters of the *Trial's* captain, John Brooke, still preserved in the India Office, London, provide us with this first authentic record. Trial Rocks, the site of the Monte Bello disaster, is named in memory of the vessel.

The *Trial* left London for Java on an expedition with an eye to East Indies trade. When she ran to her doom on a shelf of rocks on the night of May 25, 1622, she had a company of 143. Of these, ninety-seven were drowned; the others made a remarkable escape in two small boats. Both managed to reach Batavia; one boat under Captain Brooke appears to have made off immediately after the wreck, but the second, commanded by the mate, Thomas Bright, remained at one of the Monte Bello Islands for a week, during which Bright made two charts of the area, but these have not survived. Incidentally, the original letters concerning the wreck were not rediscovered until the late 1920s.

The various lagoons of the Monte Bello group (the islands were named by Nicholas Baudin in 1802 in honour of the Duke of Montebello) have been used from time to time as harbours by pearling and whaling vessels, and an unsuccessful attempt was made in the 1930s to establish a factory on Hermite Island for canning fish and turtle flesh.

Few of Western Australia's islands are inhabited and, after leaving Rottnest, one has to travel to the far north-west coast to reach an island township. The only inhabited island between Rottnest and Cockatoo Island in Yampi Sound is Dirk Hartog, the most westerly point in Australia. It was here, in 1616, that the Dutchman set up his inscribed pewter plate recording his visit to what he thought was an arid island. The plate was left on the northernmost promontory, which was named Cape Inscription by a French expedition in 1801. A lighthouse now stands on the cape, and to it has been fixed a brass plate commemorating Dirk Hartog's landing.

If Dirk could come back today he would be surprised to see that the 'arid' island is now an entire sheep station, the sea serving as a natural boundary fence. And he surely would be equally surprised to learn that this finger-shaped island 48 miles long and 3 to 7 miles wide, surrounded by the salt sea, has excellent fresh water, obtained by merely sinking a 30-foot bore. Although there is not much grass on the island the sheep feed mainly on scrub. The members of the little community have to travel 25 miles in a small boat to reach the nearest township, Denham.

Cockatoo Island in Yampi Sound is part of the Buccaneer Archipelago, one of the most dangerous areas on the west coast for mariners. The archipelago comprises four groups of small islands through which a violent tide rip runs at up to 10 knots, creating hazardous whirlpools. It was named by Lieutenant Phillip King when surveying the coast in 1821, after the English buccaneer William Dampier, who landed somewhere in the vicinity in 1688.

Yampi Sound's many islands include the rich iron-ore Cockatoo. The name Yampi is derived from a native word meaning fresh water, and Cockatoo Island was so named because in past years it was the home of flocks of tens of thousands of white cockatoos. Today, the presence of man has driven most of the birds elsewhere, and the flocks have greatly diminished in numbers.

A mere ten miles square, the tiny rugged island is composed almost entirely of high-grade iron-ore whose wealth is valued at millions of pounds. Cockatoo is doing a major job in expanding Australia's steel industry and the Commonwealth's prosperity. Some 500 people live and work on this remote and secluded island. Surrounded by precipitous cliffs rising to heights of 470 feet, there is little soil and Cockatoo lacks softening foliage, but the scenery is dramatic and all the homes in the township site have magnificent views of the vivid blue sea of Yampi Sound dotted with islands of ever-changing hues.

The iron-ore deposits were discovered as far back as 1880, but no attempt to exploit the resources was made until the years preceding World War II. In 1945 preparations were begun for mechanical extraction. This entailed the construction of roads up steep cliff-faces, the setting-up of a prefabricated town, and the building of an exceptionally long jetty with a floating head, in order to compensate for the great tidal range in the area. The first shipment of iron-ore reached Port Kembla, N.S.W., in 1951, and to date about six million tons have been extracted. Millions more lie there waiting for the huge electric shovels to bite into it.

Lack of fresh water is a problem on Cockatoo, and the ships that take away the ore bring back fresh water in ballast. A community garden in the township square gives the atmosphere and colour one generally associates with northern islands. Hibiscus and bougainvillea of flamboyant hues mingle with coconut palms, paw-paw and other tropical trees. The home sites are located on an isthmus between Yampi Sound and the open sea and thus enjoy continuous cooling

14

breezes. Glorious weather prevails on the island from about May to October with temperatures in the 70s and 80s, but for the rest of the year — during the wet season — recordings soar to the 90s with high humidity.

The Broken Hill Proprietary Company Ltd., which leases the island, built the township and the all-electric homes fitted with modern refrigerators, hot-water service and cooking appliances. The Yampi Recreation Club is the popular rendezvous for residents and there is a fine swimming pool, tennis courts and open-air movies. The cost of living on Cockatoo is surprisingly moderate, and almost everything can be bought there at Perth retail prices. A primary school looks after the education of youngsters, but correspondence lessons are necessary for the older ones. After two years on the island, all employees of B.H.P. together with their families are eligible for six weeks' holiday plus their return fares to Perth. A small coaster, *Yampi Lass,* makes a weekly voyage from Cockatoo Island to Derby, ninety miles south, carrying passengers, mail and cargo. The island is also connected with Fremantle by a monthly shipping service.

Koolan Island, which is adjacent to Cockatoo, is of similar geological composition, and work has begun to develop its iron-ore riches. The Queen and the Duke of Edinburgh touched the most remote spot of their 1963 Australian tour when they landed on Koolan Island, the furthest outpost of the Australian steel industry. Their one-hour visit to Koolan, which expects few visitors, much less Royalty, caused a mass migration from the sister island of Cockatoo. Practically the whole 650 population of Yampi Sound were assembled on Koolan for the Royal welcome. A sea and air lift carried more than 300 people the seven miles from Cockatoo to Koolan, and the former island was deserted for the first time since iron production began in 1951.

B.H.P.'s organization is on the American pattern and is almost entirely based on sea transport. Apart from the islands of Cockatoo and Koolan, iron-ore is obtained from rich coastal deposits in South and Western Australia and conveyed by the company's own fleet direct to Newcastle and Port Kembla, N.S.W. There, with the aid of coke and limestone, the ore is reduced in blast furnaces to pig-iron. Molten iron is transferred to open-hearth furnaces, mixed with steel scrap, and converted to steel. This steel, after passing through rolling mills, emerges in various shapes and sizes as finished products.

3

The Missionary Islands

AN AMBITIOUS programme of development has recently been announced for mission islands along the coast of Arnhem Land in the Northern Territory. This programme involves the expenditure of approximately £1 million over the next five years in housing, education facilities, also for development of fishing, agriculture, timber, and beef, for the general well-being of the aboriginal inhabitants of the area. The Methodist mission islands comprise Croker, Goulburn, Milingimbi in the Crocodile Islands group, and Elcho Island. Two Catholic mission islands in the same area are Bathurst and Melville. A visitor to any of these mission island cannot help being impressed by the activity and development going on.

The whole of Croker Island is held as a mission lease, where at the Methodist mission station on its eastern side part-aborigines are taught farming, stock-raising and other occupations that will help them to become self-supporting. The island, 200 miles north-east of Darwin, is some 27 miles long and in the south rises to about 200 feet. Well over 200 children have passed through Croker Island, attending school there, and after reaching eighteen, moved into Darwin or elsewhere to seek employment.

The settlement is developed on a cottage system, each with its 'mother' and run like an ordinary home. The children have their own chores around the cottage, help plan the daily meals, and cope with the laundry and other household problems. They also go for the 'messages' at a central store. Just as in a family group, each cottage has children of dif-

17

ferent age groups, the older ones looking after the younger children.

Croker Island mission is equipped with sporting fields and material and the older children are taught office work, domestic arts and woodwork. More than 700 head of beef and cattle graze on the island, which is well watered and has a good stream about one mile from the settlement. Paw-paws, pineapples, limes and even mushrooms flourish on Croker, and fish, oysters, crayfish, crabs and turtles are plentiful in the surrounding waters.

In former years these waters were a rendezvous for Macassar trepangers, and the South Australian Government once maintained a customs station on the island, of which Alfred Search, author of several books of Northern Territory reminiscences, was at one time in charge. In the 1890s aborigines from Croker Island paddled their canoes to Point Brogden, 40 miles to the east, and killed the shipwrecked crew of a Macassar boat.

Goulburn Island is one of a group of two islands both so named, although the official name of the missionary one is South Goulburn Island. Both are believed to have been sighted by Abel Tasman in 1644; they were named in 1818 by Phillip King in honour of the Under-Secretary for the Colonies, Henry Goulburn. While King was examining the islands in 1818, and again in 1819, he was attacked by the island aborigines.

Unlike Croker Island, the Goulburn mission is a full-blooded native settlement. The island covers an area of about 30 square miles and is separated from the mainland at Ross Point by Macquarie Strait, 1½ miles in width. At the rear of the mission is a memorial coconut grove to Reverend Leonard Kentish who was caught by the Japanese during the war and later executed in the Aru Islands. Mr Kentish was sailing from Goulburn Island to another mission when a Japanese seaplane swooped down and bombed and strafed his boat. The seaplane landed and Mr Kentish was dragged out of the water and taken prisoner.

To help support the missionary work on Goulburn, the

natives make baskets and mats from the leaves of the pandanus trees on the island and these are sold in southern cities. One of the natives is 54-year-old Michael, a gifted wood-carver, whose work has won high praise in art circles.

Milingimbi Island is another full-blood settlement and a hive of activity. Its good earth produces peanuts, maize, and many varieties of vegetables and tropical fruits. Lucerne is grown to feed the 300-odd cattle, including dairy cows, during the dry season. The natives have built themselves a fine church making extensive use of adobe brick. The red adobe comes from soil and gravel quarried in a wartime R.A.A.F. pit and may be seen in many of the native houses and other buildings.

Just as the making of adobe bricks for building material seems to be the main occupation on Milingimbi, so the sawmill on Elcho Island is the keynote of native activity. The origin of the name of Elcho is obscure. The 30 miles long and up to 9 miles wide island is a depot for the Methodist Overseas Missions' two £12,000 35-ton motor vessels serving their four islands and one mainland mission settlement. The timber industry on Elcho is followed by fishing and farmlets. The sawmill turns out some 4,500 super feet of cypress pine each month and the logs are floated across from the mainland to be cut up.

Fishing is a big industry and the mission has carried out experiments with shark fertilizer in an endeavour to overcome the nitrogen deficiency of Elcho's soil. In 1925 a series of bores for oil were sunk on the island but the project was unsuccessful. A so-called pitch lake there is, in fact, merely a spring with an iridescent scum on its surface. Small farms, about half an acre each, are run by the natives, and the families are self-sufficient, supplementing their farm produce with sea foods and wild life delicacies.

Elcho Island does not depend on the missionary boats for mainland communication. A DC3 plane of the MacRobertson Miller Airline provides a regular service and the arrival and departure of the plane is always a social event. The friendly natives stream down to the grass airstrip, flanking both sides of it. Welcoming or farewelling the gleaming plane, they always cheer if some of the passengers are members of their own tribe.

It is in Arnhem Land that aboriginal art has developed to the highest level, and wonderful examples may be seen on the mission islands of Melville and Bathurst. Here can be found grave posts and ceremonial posts 20 feet high, a remarkable range of sacred totemic symbols, bark coffins, log drums, twined baskets, weapons, paddles and ornaments bearing complex and artistic, many-coloured designs. The bark paintings from Arnhem Land are now recognized as one of the most outstanding forms of primitive art in the world. In north-eastern Arnhem Land they portray remarkable compositions, covering the whole surface of the bark sheet, and they incorporate totemic animals and plants, ancestral beings (many of which are snakes), clouds of various kinds, rain, waves and other natural features, as well as sea and sky associated with the totems or legends.

Most of the subjects are simple landscapes embodying things that are of interest to the native from a ritual or economic point of view. These designs, which may be sacred subjects, may also be painted on the chests of initiated men. Many non-sacred paintings on bark are simply pictures of hunting and fishing grounds, mortuary rites, camp dances, boats and daily activities; these may be painted by any of the men. On Groote Eylandt, an island lying in the Gulf of Carpentaria with a mission station run by the Church Missionary Society, totemic animals as single figures predominate in the bark paintings, but compositions explaining the legends are also depicted.

The aborigine does not begin his art career until he is initiated as a warrior, usually in his late youth or early adult life. This is the stage at which he enters the world of sacred mythology and ceremonial. His aesthetic inclinations are given impetus. He learns the significance of the designs. He may use weapons that bear them or he may see sacred objects.

The aborigine is a natural artist, completely absorbed and joyful in the performance of ceremonies and corroborees and in the making and decorating of weapons. He appreciates a 'pretty fella' piece of work just as we do, but his artistic talent has become so interwoven with other aspects of his life that function, rather than beauty or originality, has become paramount in his art. Each of the totemic groups of various clans has its own art pattern with a song or myth in which its magical power lies. The song is chanted when the design is being applied to any object, or when a sacred emblem is being displayed. This is all part of the aborigine's desire to establish a beneficial relationship with his environment.

It was necessary for me to obtain permission from Bishop O'Loughlin of Darwin to visit Bathurst and Melville Islands. When I called on His Lordship in July 1962 he was working as a labourer in the grounds of the almost completed Memorial Cathedral. A large working bee, some of them non-Catholics, were generously giving their spare time to ensure that this truly majestic example of contemporary neo-gothic architecture would be ready for the opening date five weeks hence. Bulldozers and lorries had been loaned free of charge by non-Catholics, and the Bishop himself, who graciously granted my request, was using a jack-hammer. Such is the grand spirit and mateship of the North.

I would have preferred to travel from Darwin to both islands by the missionary lugger *Margaret Mary*, but its infrequent trips did not coincide with my itinerary so I journeyed the 60-odd miles by charter plane.

The people of Bathurst and Melville Islands are fundamentally of the same ethnical group as the natives of the mainland of Arnhem Land, although there are differences of language and considerable variation in ornaments, weapons and tattoo marks. Also the marriage laws differ. Physically, these island people are rather short and thick-set with crinkly hair, like the Papuans, while the mainland people tend to be taller, slimmer and their hair is straight.

Bathurst and Melville Islands are separated from each other by Apsley Strait, a channel 50 miles long and a mile

21

wide, affected by a rip tide. Bathurst Island was first sighted, in 1644, by Abel Tasman, who believed it to be part of the mainland. It was not until 1819 that Phillip King proved the two islands to be separated from each other and from the mainland, and he named Bathurst Island after Earl Bathurst. Melville was named in honour of Viscount Melville, First Lord of the Admiralty.

Both islands are large ones. Bathurst has an area of more than 1,000 square miles while Melville is a big crescent of 2,240 square miles. Two priests and four nuns look after the mission on Bathurst Island, the natives being all full-bloods. They are healthy and well cared for and are taught useful occupations; the women are renowned for their beautiful needlework. Nevertheless, the priests are somewhat concerned for the future of the men as there is little demand for their services. Not that the natives have any desire to leave their idyllic home for Darwin or elsewhere on the mainland, and those who do always want to return.

Praiseworthy is the policy of the missionaries in preserving and encouraging the aborigines' art and culture in its many forms. The natives of Bathurst Island are skilled dancers and singers, and I saw and heard remarkable examples of their artistry in song and dance. Shortly after my visit to Bathurst Island the Australian Elizabethan Trust decided to stage an 'Aboriginal Theatre' in the southern capital cities, and director Stefan Haag chose a group of these natives aged from sixteen to sixty.

Many aboriginal dances and songs have been performed possibly for thousands of years. For instance, starting an incalculable number of centuries ago, every time a Bathurst Islander has seen the shadowy craters of the moon he has thought of and often danced out (as did twenty of them in Sydney and Melbourne) the beautiful and haunting legend of Purukupali and Waiei. It was Brother Howley, a Bathurst Island missionary, who told me the story:

Purukupali and Waiei lived with their young son in the dream time. One day Purukupali left his wife and went walkabout, and the moon, Tupara, came down and wooed Waiei. She left the child and went off with Tupara. Puruku-

22

Cockatoo Island, Western Australia, is composed almost entirely of iron ore

*Grave poles depict the dead man's life history, Melville Island,
Northern Territory*

pali returned from his walkabout and was horrified to find his son dead of neglect. He and Tupara duelled with fighting sticks and Tupara, beaten, was banished to the sky, where his wounds are still visible. Purukupali took his dead son and walked into the sea, never to return. The repentant Waiei mourned and wept and collapsed in grief on the shores of the island. She woke as a bird, a curlew, and to this day walks the beaches, wailing.

Another dance creation, by contrast, had its inspiration as late as World War II. Since 1942 the Bathurst Islanders have told — with the chanting, mime, claps, shuffles and leaps that characterize the corroboree — the story of the sixty-five Japanese air raids on Darwin. In this vivid corroboree one native becomes an aircraft spotter, using his rhythm sticks as field-glasses, another, with hands over ears, mimes a radio operator, and a third uses a spear as an anti-aircraft gun. Dancers, with outstretched arms, 'fly' around the harried defenders, bombing, and being shot down.

There is an inescapable lilt in aboriginal singing, the lifting of one note on to the next, but they have a trueness of pitch — so much so that the white man's tempered piano throws them out. They perform much better unaccompanied, and are at their best in their own native songs. Always they sing with great feeling even with alien songs whose words are beyond the scope of their experience.

To watch the Bathurst Islanders in their dance interpretations, accompanied by songmen, didgeridoo and singing-sticks is an unforgettable experience. Having seen such famed male dancers as America's Ted Shawn, Spain's fiery Luisillo, and stars of the Bolshoi Ballet, I yet found the primitive dancing of these aborigines to be even more exciting. Ted Shawn made a special visit to the North to watch their interpretations and said that the world could offer no finer dancing. The natives' litheness, astonishingly quick movements and agility are breathtaking. Dancing and miming are part of their ageless inheritance.

Under the coconut palms of Bathurst Island I watched a group of young boys perform a kangaroo corroboree that was a masterpiece of dance realism. Cleverly made-up with grey daubings of clay and tufts of kangaroo fur, they mimed the animals' every movement in an amazingly life-like manner. The sensitive twitching of the nostrils, the paws scratching the face, the feeding among the herbage, the loping hops of the animals, the sudden alertness for danger: all this was uncannily conveyed in a completely satisfying art form. It seemed incredible that young boys could weave such magical make-believe.

The whole scene was interpreted to the accompaniment of a quartet of didgeridoos and rhythm or music sticks. There again, the players were young boys. Having a didgeridoo of my own (obtained from Groote Island), but never having mastered the playing of it, I took the opportunity of asking one of the boys to give me a lesson. The lad was so expert he could raise and lower the tone of the instrument — something I thought quite impossible — and he was eager to teach me. Even with such a master I made no progress, much to the mirth of the native onlookers. My lungs could not cope with the breath control needed to sustain the eerie droning.

Few Australians are aware that the didgeridoo is unknown to aborigines of the mainland. The most primitive of musical instruments, it is merely a piece of bamboo or a hollow sapling, about five feet in length, treated by soaking in water and smearing with grease to improve the tone. Special ceremonial varieties of the didgeridoo (my own is one of them) vary from ten to fifteen feet long and are rich in tribal decorations.

Later I was to see magnificent dance interpretations by adult Bathurst Islanders, including vivid studies of hunting scenes and death rituals for the driving out of evil spirits from the corpse. The 'corpse' was no mere prop, as white dancers would use, but a native who kept absolutely motionless despite the complex ceremonies and purification handling to which he was subjected.

These aborigines have an inborn dignity that whites might envy. Thus, when a leader of one dance group lost his very brief loin cloth while executing a particularly vigorous movement he yet retained his dignity — and resourcefulness. Stark naked, he quickly dropped to the ground and began to improvise swaying body movements in harmony with the other dancers whilst he somehow managed to adjust his g-string. Then he was on his feet again and once more the leader. I must admit, however, that a little of his wild abandonment was missing and a slight tension was apparent as though he anticipated further strip-tease trouble.

Unlike Bathurst, all the natives on Melville Island are half-castes and those of any mixed bloods. The work for these people was begun by Father Connors, M.S.C., in 1940, following the Government's adoption of a policy to remove all half-castes of Australian aboriginal and of white, Japanese or Polynesian descent from the natives' camps and place them in the care of the various missions. Father Connors planned to make the settlement on Melville Island self-supporting, despite the fact that 100 years previously a British garrison was established on the same island but was abandoned mainly because of scurvy sickness. The garrison leader, in his diary, spoke of the foul, malignant climate and said that it was impossible to grow fruits and vegetables in the sterile soil.

Father Connors proved the fallacy of this belief by establishing farms on a thoroughly scientific basis at a place fittingly named Garden Point. The country around the mission headquarters looks like a luxuriant tropical garden. At the time of my visit there were long rows of paw-paw trees heavy with fruit, and many orange, lemon and mandarin trees. I saw, too, crops of sugar cane, peanuts, the choicest of cashew nuts, melons, custard apples, bananas, figs — the list could go on interminably. Around a crystal spring were growing nine different varieties of sweet potatoes, beans, radishes, tomatoes, and a field of rice. And to all this could be added fresh eggs, milk and delicacies from the sea to tempt even a city gourmet.

Strolling along the pure white sands of the fine beach near the mission, to top off a swim in the clear waters of the Arafura Sea, I found the gentle cooling breeze refreshing after the heat and humidity of Darwin. Afterwards I questioned the mission nuns about the all-year-round climate, bearing in mind that the first official report had described it as 'foul and malignant'. They assured me that the island climate was an ideal one, healthy and mild without the extremes of dry and wet temperature encountered on the mainland.

Father Flynn, M.S.C., a lay brother and six nuns form the staff of the Catholic mission which is known as Our Lady of Victories. The schoolchildren are taught trades to prepare them for life back on the mainland; the more talented go to Darwin for special training. But above all, Fr. Flynn told me, Melville Island (its native name is Yermalner) is meant to be a home. When the boys and girls grow up, they marry the partners of their choice. They live on at the mission until their family life is stable enough to stand the stresses of life in outside communities. Once stabilised, the families are free to move out and fend for themselves.

Strangely enough, there are always more girls than boys on Melville Island. So those who do not marry must move back to the mainland to settle. Questioning the girls I found that few of them want to leave, and I was not surprised when they told me they are happy to stay where they are.

The school is a handsome modern building of tropical-style architecture, its classrooms being furnished with better appointments and facilities than those generally seen even in city primary schools. An artistic ornamental fountain graces the entrance, and a small plaque on it mentions that the stones at the base were made by convicts and had been taken from the ruins of the ill-fated Fort Dundas settlement on the island. Scarcely a trace remains today of that unfortunate venture.

Melville Islanders are famous for the beautiful carved and decorated grave posts they make for their dead. These may be seen near the Government native settlement at Snake Bay on the north coast of the island. Here the natives celebrate the end of the mourning period for a dead man with a Puckamini corroboree, which dramatizes the story of his life and death.

A family often has to save up for a long time to pay for the Puckamini, because they have to pay not only the carvers who depict the dead man's life history on the poles, but also the song-men who give the story of his life in sound at the ceremony of planting the poles around the grave. The corroboree usually lasts for several days. While a Puckamini is in preparation — which may take months, as the poles have to be carved and then painted — the chief mourners, the song-men, must not wash or handle food. Their meals have to be fed to them by some relation. The children like to try their hand at painting and carving. They make miniature Puckamini poles on which they carve birds and animals.

There are several white families at the settlement grouped around Snake Bay. Most of the native men are employed at the sawmill, and the women weave mats and baskets. The white families are housed in modern flats with their own lighting plant. Some of the islanders are in neat cottages, some still live in fairly primitive conditions.

'It's a good life on Melville Island for both white inhabitants and aboriginal,' said Mrs Alan Ingram, the wife of the agricultural manager. 'We women go fishing, and the men go crocodile shooting. There are excellent oysters and crabs which the natives bring along with their big nippers very neatly tied, thank goodness. We eat quite a lot of fish,' added Mrs Ingram, 'especially Spanish mackerel, trevally and barramundi. You see, our meat supplies only come in once a fortnight.'

The sister-in-charge of the premises used as a hospital said that the aborigines' favourite remedies are headache tablets as a cure-all, 'rubbim medicine' (linament) and cough medicine. The Government plans to build a small hospital to replace the premises now being used — one end of a repair and maintenance shed. 'Humans get mended at one end,' said Sister Schroeder, 'and vehicles at the other.

'Our biggest problem,' she explained, 'is diagnosis. However, we can speak to the Flying Doctor on the radio and get expert advice, and we have a routine medical visit every five or six weeks.' Sister Schroeder admires her patients. 'The aborigines are a very happy crowd, with a great sense of humour, and very dramatic in their mourning.'

It was in 1824 that the British Government chose Melville Island for the first attempt to establish a military settlement on the north coast of Australia. The area was named Fort Dundas, and under the leadership of Captain J. J. Bremer building began as soon as the expedition arrived. A fort was constructed, 75 yards by 50 yards, and surrounded by a ditch. On October 21, 1824 (the anniversary of the battle of Trafalgar), the colours were hoisted on the fort and a royal salute was fired from two 9-pounder guns and four 18-pounder carronades.

The post suffered a succession of misfortunes. Those who went any distance from the fort were harassed by hostile aborigines, and dissension and sickness disrupted the settlement. Supply ships failed to arrive as promised, and so unsatisfactory were reports of the Fort Dundas settlement that the Colonial Office decided in 1826 to abandon it.

At this period the population of the settlement was 115 males (54 of them convicts), six women, and 14 members of ships' crews; the stock consisted of 16 cattle, 23 sheep and lambs, 54 swine, and 16 buffaloes from Timor. Three acres of land were under cultivation and a total of 52 acres had been cleared. It was not until three years later, however, that the stock and stores were removed to a new post at Raffles Bay on the mainland (this, too, was abandoned a few months later), and the people to Sydney.

4

The King and the Bishop

BATHURST and Melville Islands were for many years the homes of two remarkable and worthy pioneers. Robert Joel Cooper, better known in the North as King Joe, ruled Melville Island as his kingdom for a generation, while Bathurst Island was for more than 40 years the headquarters of Bishop Francis Xavier Gsell, famous as 'The Bishop with 150 Wives'.

King Joe was the only white man ever to become the absolute ruler of a tribe of aborigines. Physically and mentally he was a fine type of Australian, upright and honourable and of commanding appearance. He stood well over six feet in height and had a remarkably keen pair of blue eyes.

Cooper arrived in the Northern Territory in 1881, having come overland from South Australia, where he was born. Utterly fearless, and straight in all his dealings, he soon won over the fierce Melville Islanders, and before long was proclaimed Chief over the Five Tribes. He was put through all the secret rites of the aborigines, and to the day of his death never revealed them to another white man.

King Joe was a man who would carry out his principles unswervingly. He was a non-smoker and a teetotaller — an exceedingly rare combination in white men who live in North Australian bush country, far removed from civilization.

Before he was chosen chief, trouble was always brewing on Melville Island. The islanders were a warlike race, avoided by both whites and natives. When Cooper took charge all this was altered. He ruled with a rod of iron, but always justly. The punishment of evil-doers he attended to personally. Wearing only a loincloth, he would take a spear, wommera and throwing-stick, and hunt down any native who had broken one of the tribal laws and had fled to escape punishment. Being a fine tracker, as well as a first-class bushman, he always returned with the offender.

For a white man to be made a chief of wild aborigines was an honour not easily won. Even when Cooper had been accepted by the tribes, two native pretenders to the 'throne' challenged him to combat. Both were powerful young athletes famed for their prowess as warriors.

Cooper accepted their challenge and prepared for a battle in which he was to fight both men in turn. Surrounded by hundreds of natives, he and his first opponent faced each other. They wore loincloths and carried only spears and a wommera each. They were separated by about 100 yards, and at a given signal each began to creep up on the other. The white man had learned to throw spears when quite a lad and was an expert in the art. However, the native knew all the tricks, too. So agile were the pair that this first test ended in a stalemate; neither drew blood.

The council of the old men of the tribe then decided that, as both were evenly skilled, they should come to grips with waddies. These weapons are about six feet in length, and shaped like a straight sword with two cutting edges. They are made from ironwood. The handle is carved to give a good grip, generally being held by both hands.

The thickness of a native's skull is abnormal; it can withstand a blow which would kill a European. Cooper was well aware of this, but so great was his confidence and fighting skill that he managed to evade the aborigine's attacks until he found his opportunity to bring home a tremendous smash on the skull of his opponent. The fight was over. Though the native was not killed, he was knocked unconscious, and the white man was proclaimed victor.

The following day was set aside for the next trial by battle, but the second challenger had lost heart and confidence, and in the first round of the spear-throwing received a wound in his left thigh which put him out of action. King Joe had established himself in the only fashion understood by his subjects. Cooper married a full-blooded native of Melville Island, who proved herself to be an excellent wife and devoted mother. She presented him with a son and two daughters.

There was hardly a dialect between Darwin and the Gulf of Carpentaria with which Robert Joel Cooper was unfamiliar. In buffalo-shooting he outclassed even America's famed Buffalo Bill. Altogether, he accounted for 27,000 buffaloes during his reign. (The buffaloes were wild descendants of those left behind when the Fort Dundas settlement was abandoned more than half a century earlier. They had multiplied tremendously in the surrounding marshes; the hides were so thick that native spears hardly dinted them and thus they escaped annihilation.) In the museum at Adelaide there is a rifle with which Cooper shot 3,000 of them.

King Joe was extremely fond of his son, Reuben. Like his father, Reuben was tall and well built, and a wonderful athlete. He was educated at Prince Alfred College, South Australia. Just before World War I the noted Australian athlete, 'Snowy' Baker, chose Reuben, with some other young outstanding sportsmen, to tour the world giving exhibitions of physical culture. Cooper senior was justly proud of this, and when the war caused the abandonment of the project he was a very disappointed man.

Before his death, the white ruler was acknowledged by all the people of the North as a man who had done more good for the former fierce Melville Island natives than anybody else who ever entered the Territory. His descendants today have proved themselves worthy children of a notable sire.

The remarkable pioneering work of the late Dr. Francis Xavier Gsell on Bathurst Island is immortalized in the book *The Bishop with 150 Wives*. In 1906, his appointment as Vicar Apostolic of Darwin made him the spiritual leader of a diocese of more than half-a-million square miles. It also launched the Doctor into a fight against sorcery, magic and primitive cruelty on Bathurst Island. He found old people and unwanted children being buried alive, and young boys at tribal initiation ceremonies drinking, and in some cases living for weeks upon the blood of ancient sufferers from yaws, tuberculosis, granuloma and even leprosy.

He beat the witch-doctors with aspirin. His fame spread throughout the island when it was learned that the easily taken little tablets cured headaches even more effectively than the witch-doctor's method of biting through a vein in the patient's forehead until flow of blood relieved the ache, and then following a lot of hocus-pocus by 'extracting' a large pebble from the sufferer's head by means of the mouth.

Under the tribal laws of Bathurst Island, all the women were the wives of the old men who had from ten to twenty wives, while the young men up to thirty or forty years of age had none at all. They could, perhaps, gain wives by heritage from deceased brothers or other relatives, but when that happened it was the custom to give the young women to the old men, and the old women to the young men. Men of sixty with wives of fifteen, and boys of fifteen with wives of sixty were common. The result was racial suicide and children were rare.

This was the set-up against which Dr. Gsell's first 'wife' rebelled when, in 1927, she fled for protection to the Catholic Mission on Bathurst Island. Neither her mother, nor her mother's mother, nor any female of her tribe had ever had any choice in the matter of marriage, but the slim, ten-year-old native girl could not face the future that had been arranged for her.

For her, the only form rebellion could take was flight and among the tribes the flights of terrified women from the wrath of their race had always ended the same way — in ceremonial slaying. But the girl won out and found not only a new hope for her tribal sisters but a chance of survival for her dying people.

Back in the scrubby ranges the tribe's trackers were busy, moving over the girl's trail with uncanny speed, followed by the armed warriors who were to carry out their code of justice. They arrived at the Mission the next morning, a fierce angry crowd. When Dr. Gsell came out to them they demanded the shivering, terrified girl. He refused, of course, but he could not reason with them. The old bridegroom jabbered and danced with rage, and the warriors with him. According to their age-old laws they believed him to be a deeply-wronged man. They raised their spears and threatened to kill this white stealer of girls.

But Dr. Gsell knew the natives, as well as he knew his duty; they might shut their ears to his words, but there are things to which they could not shut their eyes. He brought out flour, tobacco, a tomahawk and coloured trinkets and placed them before the natives. Their anger gave way to eager curiosity. When the priest offered to buy the girl in honest trade from the man to whom she had been promised, there was no hesitation. The warriors went back to the ranges, filled with goodwill and a little envy of the old man who had been able to exchange a mere girl for such treasures. So it was that the bishop gained the first of the 'wives' whose number was to grow to 150 in the following eighteen years.

Bishop Gsell, Father Henschke (his Vicar General) and their assistants were happiest when they were marrying one of the bishop's 'wives' to one of the Christian boys at the Mission and they have performed the ceremony many times, with fine results. Whatever the position with less fortunate tribes, the depopulation of Bathurst Island was stopped and there are many native families of up to eight or ten children belonging to couples who have been able to marry when both were young and fond of each other.

A memorial to Bishop Gsell is erected not on Bathurst but at Paru village across the strait on Melville Island. The natives have built it themselves, and it consists of a concrete cairn set in the centre of a gravel path which is in the shape of a cross. The memorial, which is surrounded by floral gardens and trees and has its own flagpole, was blessed by Father John Fallon, M.S.C., in 1963, on April 11 — the anniversary of the date that Bishop Gsell landed on Melville Island in 1911 when he was seeking a site for a mission.

Father Fallon, a good-looking young six-footer from my own parish in Sydney, told me that after the memorial blessing the natives present gathered round the 'old men' of the tribe and heard stories about the Bishop and his grand work in the days of savagery on the islands.

Government assistance to the various Christian mission societies on these northern islands and the mainland has been generous. Missionary efforts in the past were often attended by disappointment (and in some cases utter failure) and called for greater Christian fortitude, patience and faith. The missionaries have come to the gradual realization that religious teaching should be supplemented by other teaching for a people whose whole way of life is being transformed. The Benedictine, Presbyterian, Methodist and Lutheran missions, to name but a few, follow the pattern of grafting on the new way of life to the old only in a very gradual long-range plan, training them for pastoral, agricultural and other pursuits.

Arnhem Land, whose mangrove-lined northern coast facing the Arafura Sea is so dotted with islands, covers an area of 31,200 square miles. This coast was first made known through the discoveries of Dutch and Portuguese mariners between the middle of the sixteenth century and the beginning of the seventeenth. It is named after the vessel *Arnhem* which in 1623 was the first to sight the north-eastern coast.

The earliest visitors to the Arnhem Land coast, which they looked upon as virtually their own domain, and which they called *Marega*, were Indonesian traders. It is believed that their first arrival was in the sixteenth or even the fifteenth century. Matthew Flinders encountered some of the praus near Elcho Island in 1803; but from all indications their visits had already been going on for generations.

In subsequent years Arnhem Land became comparatively well known during the latter phase of Malay-Macassan contact, and during the establishment of European settlements. Later came attempts to settle this part of the Northern Territory, and to exploit its waters for marine products. Japanese and other Asiatics also took part in pearling opera-

34

tions. Christian mission stations were established gradually at various places all around the Arnhem Land coast. Only the missions remain and the whole vast region has been since 1931 an aboriginal reserve.

The name of Arnhem Land was formerly applied to all the northern part of the Territory, from the Roper River west to the Victoria River; but today it refers only to the reserve, one of the largest in Australia, lying east and south-east of Darwin. The heart of Arnhem Land with its gorges, mountains, swamps and rocky plains, is only partially explored. Most of the aborigines prefer to live in the fertile areas bordering the coast, where even in bad seasons food is plentiful and fresh water is comparatively easy to find. Despite its extent, the population of Arnhem Land has been assessed at only about 4,000, including aborigines on mission stations.

A group of seven islands in the waters of Arnhem Land are known as English Company's Islands. They were first sighted by the *Arnhem,* and in 1803, nearly two hundred years later, they were visited by Matthew Flinders. Inglis Island, the largest of the group, is 14 miles long by up to 3 miles wide. Flinders named the islands 'mostly after gentlemen in the East India directory; and in compliment to that respectable body of men, whose liberal attention to this voyage was useful to us and honourable to them, the whole cluster is named the English Company's Islands'.

Although most of the islands are rather bare, a valley on Cotton Island took the fancy of Flinders, and he wrote that it 'might be a delightful situation for a college of monks, who could bear the heat of the climate and were impenetrable to the stings of musketoes'.

Of all the islands off the coast of Arnhem Land there are none with more interesting examples of aboriginal rock paintings than the Wessel Islands in the north-east. North Wessel is renowned for its Cave of the Rainbow Serpent, a great rock recess in which is painted a strikingly coloured representation of a serpent with a forked tail. Early Dutch maps showed this group of islands under the name of Wessel, and when Matthew Flinders visited them in 1803 he endorsed the Dutch name. However, he named three of the islands within the group, Cunningham Islands, in honour of Captain Charles Cunningham, R.N.

Extensive deposits of bauxite lie on these islands awaiting development of the North. Prospecting on one of the Wessel group was begun in 1950, but because other deposits were found on the mainland shortly afterwards, the island mineral riches were not exploited.

5

Islands of the Gulf

LOOKING at a map of the Gulf of Carpentaria, one cannot help but notice the many Dutch names. Vanderlin Island, Duyfken Point, Sweers Island, Cape Van Diemen — all indicate visits by the early Dutch explorers and navigators. Even the Gulf itself is named after Pieter Carpentier, Governor-General of the Dutch East Indies (1622-8).

The Gulf of Carpentaria, that deep indentation on the northern coast of Australia, partly in Queensland and partly in the Northern Territory, has scarcely changed since the little Dutch vessel *Duyfken* sailed into it in 1605. Indeed, most of it is the same today as when it was first sighted by Europeans. Because of the lack of settlement in the Gulf country, a considerable part of the coastline has not been surveyed since the explorations of Matthew Flinders and John Stokes in 1803 and 1841 respectively. The gulf is 300 miles wide at its mouth and extends more than 400 miles southward to its head; as far as is known no part of its waters is more than 43 fathoms deep. The shallow waters from 3 to 10 miles offshore make navigation a dangerous undertaking for anyone but skippers of small vessels with extensive local knowledge.

When the *Duyfken,* under the command of William Jansz, entered the Gulf of Carpentaria she sailed along the eastern shore as far as Cape Keer-weer. This discovery was followed up by Jan Carstensz, who with the ships *Pera* and *Arnhem* in 1623 penetrated almost to the head of the Gulf and gave it its present name. Cape Arnhem is the boundary line on the north-west.

37

In the 400-miles coastline of the gulf there are only two small ports — Normanton and Burketown. Both are at the head of the gulf where there are extensive mud flats and mangrove swamps, and both are outlets for small shipments of pastoral produce from the interior of Queensland to ports on the north coast.

The western shore of Carpentaria is hilly and well-wooded and it is off this shore that lie the chief islands of the gulf. Some of them, like the Sir Edward Pellew Group, are uninhabited. In 1923, when H.M.S. *Geranium* made a survey of the group, an obelisk was erected on Observation Island to the memory of Matthew Flinders. Groote Eylandt is an aboriginal reserve with a mission station under the charge of the Church Missionary Society. The island measures roughly 40 miles from north to south and from 20 to 40 miles from east to west, and is thickly wooded in the interior where it rises to about 600 feet at Central Hill. There are a number of reefs and islets off its shores. Chasm Island, off the northern end of Groote, takes its name from the chasms that dissect its uppermost cliffs, in which are many caves containing remarkable examples of aboriginal art. When Matthew Flinders circumnavigated Groote Eylandt (Great Island) in 1803 he recorded traces of visits by Macassar trepang fishermen.

The bark paintings from Groote Eylandt have become world famous. In 1961-62 a collection of them was taken on a world tour for exhibition in the capital cities and created tremendous interest. Made from bark removed from the tree, and straightened by being placed upon a fire and when very hot placed on sandy ground, the paintings are truly primitive. When cold and quite flat the bark is cut to the size required. It is then painted over with black ochre, using a piece of bark as a paintbrush. Ochres of various colours are found in the bush, and mixed with water as required. After the base is complete, it is rubbed over with the juice from an orchid to 'set' the colour.

Then the actual drawing commences. The basic lines are drawn from memory with a fine piece of bark. Then a feather is used to draw in the details, and these are done with great care, giving time to colours chosen and fineness of lines. All kinds of marine life, animals, birds, people and aboriginal lore known only to the native himself are incorporated in paintings. They are sometimes painted in sets, comprising a 'dream' by the painter, and these are imaginative and unusual. It is not surprising to find sometimes twenty or more paintings of the one 'story' each passing on to a different phase in the tale.

Lying at the head of the Gulf of Carpentaria is a group of islands called Wellesley and comprising Mornington — the largest of the group — Sweers, Bentinck, the Bountiful Islands, the Forsyth Islands, and smaller islets and reefs. The group was first visited by Matthew Flinders in the *Investigator* in 1802, and named by him after the second Earl of Mornington, afterwards the first Marquis Wellesley, Governor-General of India.

Mornington Island has a splendid jetty which was built in a unique manner. For some years a good strong jetty had been badly needed but, through lack of money, the missionaries there were unable to purchase the necessary materials. They got over the difficulty by asking the children attending the mission school to bring with them every morning a stone. The children entered wholeheartedly into the scheme, and every day for months the little aborigines of all ages marched into school carrying stones of various shapes and sizes held over their heads. The stones were then taken over to the site of the proposed jetty, and in this unusual manner sufficient material was obtained to build it. The missionaries, with the help of the native men, did the building. Eighty feet long and ten feet wide, the jetty, since it was built, has withstood some of the fiercest cyclones and storms ever known in the Gulf of Carpentaria.

The island is also unique with its parachute mail. Every Christmas the children at the Mornington Island Mission joyfully watch their presents come floating down from the sky. So completely isolated is the island that at Christmas time the Commonwealth Government sees to it that the little mission is not forgotten. From the Australian mainland a plane flies over the island and drops by parachute not only any letters addressed to the mission but also toys and gifts for the hundred or more children there. The island is the only place in Australia with a parachute mail.

Until recent years Bentinck Island, named after another Governor-General of India, Lord William Bentinck, was inhabited by a primitive tribe of aborigines. The area covers some 63 square miles. In 1841 Captain J. Lort Stokes, of H.M.S. *Beagle,* observed that these aborigines used only rough rafts of sticks when crossing to adjacent islands; unlike natives on the mainland, they did not employ bark canoes or hollowed-out logs. Their dwellings were extremely primitive, and consisted merely of semi-circular barriers of grass about 2 feet high and 6 or 8 feet in diameter, arranged to face the prevailing wind. Tribal murder, combined with sickness and malnutrition, caused the numbers of the natives gradually to diminish, and in 1948 a handful of survivors was evacuated by the authorities to the mission station on Mornington Island.

Sweers Island is the most south-easterly of the Wellesley Islands group, and is 5 square miles in area. Investigator Road, between it and Bentinck Island, is the only anchorage for vessels during both monsoon and trade-wind seasons; partly for this reason, and partly because of the supposed unhealthiness of Burketown on the mainland, the Queensland Government originally intended to establish the port for the Gulf of Carpentaria on Sweers Island. A customs-house was built and a site for the proposed township of Carnarvon was surveyed, but the project was abandoned.

Matthew Flinders visited the island during his voyage on the *Investigator* and obtained much-needed water supplies by sinking a well. Wishing to perpetuate the fact that the Dutch were the earliest explorers of this part of the coast, he named Sweers Island after Salamon Sweers, a member of the Batavia Council which gave Abel Tasman his instructions in 1642. Flinders left a record of his visit by carving the name of the ship and date on a small tree, a portion of which still remained in the early years of the present century at Point Inscription.

The tree already had cut into it the ideographs of members of a Chinese junk and names and dates of other early vessels who called there, including the name of the Dutch ship *Loury* with the year 1781. When the tree showed signs of decay the limb bearing the Flinders inscription was carefully cut down and taken to the Queensland Museum in Brisbane. While at Sweers Island, Flinders noted in his log-book that he saw some sixty Malay prahus engaged in trepang and beche-de-mer fishing around the waters.

A floating lighthouse known as the *Carpentaria* is moored in the lonely waters of the Gulf of Carpentaria. When first moored in the Gulf, a keeper was left on board to take care of the light; he was to be relieved at the end of six months. But when the supply ship arrived at the end of that time no trace of the keeper could be found. It was believed that he must have been washed overboard during a storm. Strangely enough, the next keeper also disappeared. No solution to the mysteries was ever discovered, and as a result of the tragedies the authorities installed an automatic, unattended light.

Today the floating beacon is the home of countless thousands of sea birds. A warning bell tolls with every motion of the boat, but the birds have become so accustomed to the bell that it never worries them. Only the rare approach of man sends them screaming and screeching into the air in a dense cloud.

6

The Torres Strait

TORRES STRAIT, the passage of water between the northern coast of Cape York Peninsula in North Queensland and the southern coast of Papua, connecting the Coral and Arafura Seas, contains numerous islands and reefs. The largest of these islands are Prince of Wales and Banks; between these two lies Thursday Island. Navigation in Torres Strait is hazardous, and many a vessel has come to grief on these islands and the reefs around them. Some of the old Spanish shipwrecks have been seen by the pearl divers and a fair amount of their treasures recovered. On Stephens Island a fisherman found a native idol which was decorated with valuable old Castilian jewellery. Then again, on Prince of Wales Island a crumbling skeleton was found, alongside of which was a huge rusty sword of ancient Spanish design. Nearby was a valuable gold goblet. Quite a number of gold coins have also been found on Booby Island.

The group of three islets known as the Murray Islands lie at the extreme northern end of the Great Barrier Reef. There is a mission on the largest of the group which comes under Queensland jurisdiction. Formerly the natives, who are of the Papuan type, were very aggressive and were responsible for the massacre of many survivors from wrecked ships. The Murray Islanders have a legend of a ship with a silver keel which was wrecked there, every person aboard being massacred. The legend is emphatic that the keel of the vessel was of solid silver — a rich prize to the finder. Unfortunately the natives have a deep, super-stitious dread of the wreck and refuse to guide treasure

42

seekers to its whereabouts. On one occasion a white official found a group of native children there using large Spanish gold pieces as counters in a game in which flat beans usually serve as this medium.

Murray Island was the scene of the wreck of the *Pandora,* the vessel which was carrying 14 of the *Bounty* mutineers arrested in Tahiti. On Bligh's arrival home in England with the news of the mutiny, the British Government promptly fitted out the frigate *Pandora* to search for the mutineers. Captain Edward Edwards, in command of the vessel, arrived in Tahiti on March 23, 1791. Even as the anchor was being lowered two of the mutineers, midshipmen Stewart and Heywood together with a seaman named Coleman came aboard and surrendered. Later, 12 others were made prisoners. Captain Edwards continued to cruise among the islands of the Tahitian group hoping to capture more of the mutineers but his prisoners informed him that they had separated into two parties and the one in charge of Fletcher Christian had sailed with their Tahitian womenfolk to an unknown destination.

When the *Pandora* set sail for England via Torres Strait the prisoners were manacled and confined to a wooden cage 11 feet by 18 — nicknamed 'Pandora's Box' — and their miserable rations were scarcely sufficient to keep them alive. Four of the mutineers were among the thirty-five people drowned when the *Pandora* was wrecked off Murray Island on August 28. The 99 survivors left the doomed frigate in four open boats and, following Bligh's journey, reached Timor. Ultimately they landed in England.

The conduct of Captain Edwards to his prisoners, both before and after the wreck of the *Pandora* at Murray Island, has been condemned as excessively brutal by historians and even by officers in the service at that time. Sir John Barrow, writing of the mutiny in 1831, said that nothing could justify the barbaric treatment to which Captain Edwards subjected his prisoners. Heywood, one of the four acquitted at the court-martial of the ten mutineers (the rest were sentenced to death), was restored to his rank, and afterwards became a distinguished officer in the service.

Among the natives of the Torres Strait, apart from the stories they tell of white men who came in ships, there is definite evidence that large groups of white men have spent much time among them. Some of the island tribes have a strangely light skin with pronounced Latin features. Moreover, Spanish words are included in their dialects.

Secreted somewhere on Moa Island is an ancient and valuable tortoise-shell idol that was once worshipped by the islanders. The idol was the famous Dog God of Moa. It was a huge and remarkable figure of a dog, about 20 feet long and 12 feet high, modelled in thick tortoise-shell. More than two hundred of the finest tortoise-shells were used in its construction. The missionaries began their work in the Torres Strait during the early 1880s. When rumours reached the natives of Moa about these strange white men who destroyed the old gods and idols, the chiefs determined to safeguard the Dog God. They carried the great idol to a secret cave and sealed up the entrance to it. Then they made a pledge never to reveal its whereabouts to any white man. Those who knew of its hiding-place are now dead, and they have taken the secret with them to the grave. It is now believed that a landslide in past years must have covered the entrance to the Dog God's home, hiding the idol forever from the prying eyes of man.

Albany Island lies four miles from the extremity of Cape York. Its area of 3 square miles is uninhabited but it was once chosen as a site for settlement. When Queensland was separated from New South Wales, in 1859, Governor Bowen recommended that a government outpost and garrison be established on Albany Island to serve as 'a harbour of refuge for shipwrecked seamen, a coaling station, and entrepôt for the shipping trade of Torres Strait and the North Pacific'. In 1863 John Jardine, police magistrate and gold commissioner at Rockhampton, Queensland, was appointed as the island's Government Resident. However, the site proved unsuitable for settlement and Jardine moved the garrison to the mainland, calling the place Somerset after the Duke of Somerset, the name that was originally to have applied to the Albany settlement. Buried on Albany Island are the remains of Thomas Wall and Charles Niblett, two of the eight men left at Weymouth Bay in 1848 by Kennedy on his ill-fated expedition along Cape York Peninsula.

Little known is the romantic Torres Strait island that was the birthplace of the great pearling industry of Australia's northern tropical seas. Forgotten, too, is the name of Captain Banner, who, in 1868, discovered the first pearls, but whose untimely death prevented him from sharing in the fortunes that were amassed by the majority of the pioneer pearlers. Today the name of that island is Warrior Island.

In the early days, Warrior Island was known by its native name of Tute. It was the home of hostile natives — noted sea warriors whose powerful fleet of huge outrigger canoes was feared throughout Torres Strait and along the coast of New Guinea. All native trading vessels travelling between New Guinea and the mainland had to pay the Warrior Islanders a 'toll' in goods before they were allowed to pass; any vessel that refused to pay was promptly sunk and the natives on board killed.

Those were the days when Kebisu, the great mamoose (chief) and his sea raiders terrorised the islands of Torres Strait and the villages of the New Guinea coast. No less celebrated in the legend and folk lore of the Torres Strait Islanders were Id, the mamoose of Murray Islands, who waged incessant warfare with Rebes, war chief of the Darnley Islanders; Kabara, chief of the Moa Islanders, and Kwoiam, warrior chief of Mabuiag.

Strangely enough, the first white men to visit Tute received an enthusiastic reception; they were the crew of a French ship which, in distress, called there in 1790 to repair a damaged rudder. The natives gave the visitors every assistance and treated the sailors like royalty. Unfortunately the Frenchmen sailed away without offering the natives anything whatsoever for their services. This unfair treatment incensed the islanders so much that from then on they attacked every white man's boat that neared their territory.

It was not warfare that finally subdued the sea warriors. In the early sixties of last century Captain Moresby of

H.M.S. *Basilisk* managed to make friends with them by giving them presents of tobacco and other trade goods when he encountered them at sea. Later, in 1868, Captain Banner happened to call at the island and was astonished to see all the natives — men, women and children — wearing strings and ornaments of valuable pearls. The children were even using pearls for marbles.

When Captain Banner's story reached civilization, the great pearl rush commenced to the then lonely and little known seas of Australia's northern coasts. Gradually the pearl-beds of Tute, or Warrior Island as it became known, were worked out, and since the year 1900 the island has been forgotten.

An aura of romantic history also surrounds the bleak little Torres Strait island called Booby. A remarkable geographical fact is that both Cook and Bligh named this island Booby without each other's knowledge, because it was in their day — and still is — the nesting place of millions of boobies, a species of gannet. Bligh of the *Bounty* passed the island during his epic ocean voyage in an open boat to Timor after the mutiny in 1789. It was then that he gave it the name of Booby, completely unaware that Cook had given it the same name nearly 20 years previously.

Visitors are infrequent to this lonely rock island whose only inhabitants are the lighthouse keepers. Booby is famous for its cave which used to be a unique post office. In the early 1800s Captain Hobson, R.N., of H.M.S. *Rattlesnake,* provided the island cave with a large box with a painted notice, POST OFFICE. Alongside it were pens and ink and a log-book. In the latter skippers of sailing vessels which had navigated the hazardous Torres Strait left accounts of their experiences for the benefit of other skippers. Captains and crews dropped their letters into the box and the captains were responsible for collecting any mail for their run.

About 1847, the New South Wales Legislative Council voted £50 for stores to be left on Booby Island for shipwrecked mariners. Passing ships often left spare stores and clothing for castaways. The log-books have vanished but the old POST OFFICE box is still there, and on the walls of the cave are scratched names of old sailing vessels and crew members.

Several island churches in Torres Strait call their congregations to worship by old ships' bells which have been retrieved from wrecks. On Yam Island, in the centre of the Torres Strait, close to where Captain Banner made the first rich discovery of pearl-shell, the natives assemble for worship to the sound of a bell from a Norwegian craft wrecked on one of the innumerable reefs in the Strait. Timber from the wreck was used to build huts on Horn Island, but the Yam Islanders salvaged the bell for their church.

Jervis Island has a ship's bell weighing 70 lb. Its inscription bears the name *Integrity* and the date 1824. That vessel was wrecked while negotiating the difficult passage between Jervis and Mulgrave Islands. A shocking fate awaited all aboard her. Canoe-loads of cannibal natives killed them and pillaged the wreck. The human heads were placed on a native shrine as a religious offering.

Darnley Island native divers located in recent years two ships several fathoms down, one lying across the other. One of the wrecks was identified from various objects brought up, including a circular brass disc which bore the name *Windhover,* a famous tea clipper of the 'eighties. In endeavouring to bring up its large bell which the islanders wanted for their church it slipped right down into the depths beyond recovery.

It was on Darnley Island where the natives held at regular periods during the South-east season a ceremony to enhance the brightness of the moon. The 'zogo-man' summoned the male community to assemble at a particular grove of wangai trees; it was customary for them to bring with them supplies of food. The zogo-man's two assistants each carried a stone, one representing 'Meb', the moon, and the other 'Gerger', the sun. The stones were taken to a cleared space where each was placed in a huge clam shell. Annointing of the stones with coconut oil followed, then 'Gerger' was coloured with special red ochre. Later came chanting and ritual dancing, concluding with a ceremonial feast. Today the two sacred stones in the giant clam shells

47

stand behind the island church. They were placed there in 1921, at the foot of a sandstone cross, as a reminder of pagan days and customs, and as a memorial to the first missionaries in Torres Strait.

Although the Torres Strait islanders had no written language until the first missionaries arrived in 1871, they had a wealth of folk-lore stories handed down from one generation to another. Such tales were told to an audience big or small squatting under the palm trees or round village fires.

On the island of Mabuiag there is a large stone near the main entrance to the missionary church, and this stone, according to native legend, originally came from inside a whale. It seems that a big whale came close to the island one day and, circling round a point, suddenly ejected this strange stone from its mouth before heading out to sea. The mysterious reddish-brown object was carefully retrieved and for very many years served its part in island magic. When the church was eventually built this relic of non-Christian days was brought in from its pagan shrine as a reminder of the pre-missionary times. The story may possibly have been born as the result of a gunboat firing an iron ball when the first white men's ships passed through these waters.

Another native folk tale of the sea concerns Stephens Island — a story which tells how the islanders first discovered the Sabay fish and its virtues. Though the official name of the island is Stephens (one of Bligh's namings), it is known to the islanders as 'Attagoy'. Encircled by reefs on which numerous ships have crashed, it is famous for its large and handsome helmet shells and its thick-bodied variety of a fish called 'Sabay'. When boiled down this spike-headed fish yields a remarkably rich white oil which the native use in cooking and for other purposes.

It is said that when the world was very young there lived on Stephens a man called Badi, who was gifted with supernatural powers over birds and fish. One day he carved a piece of wood into the shape of a fish and threw it into the sea. Immediately the carving developed into a school of live fish unlike any other variety seen in these waters.

Raising a spear, Badi took aim and transfixed one of the fish as the school came closer inshore. After cooking the fish in a bailer shell he cut it into small portions and threw them to the Torres Strait pigeons hovering round. When Badi saw that the birds relished the fish and showed no harmful effects, he risked a few mouthfuls himself. 'Proper good this one!' was his verdict, and off he went to inform his people of the luscious fish he had created and to assure them that there would be a good supply for all time.

The mythical benefactor is commemorated on Stephens Island with a large memorial stone called Badi. And, indeed, the islanders (many of the males bear the name 'Sabay') will show you with pride the very stone fireplace where Badi cooked his first Sabay. Two roughly-hewn stones on either side represent the white pigeons on which the cooked fish was tested.

The principal passage in Torres Strait is Prince of Wales Channel, to the north of Goode Island; Endeavour Strait, between Prince of Wales Island and the mainland of Queensland, which was named by Captain Cook after his own ship in 1770, is seldom used nowadays except by small local boats. Torres Strait itself was named by Alexander Dalrymple, an eminent British hydrographer, on a chart published in 1767, in honour of Luis Vaez de Torres, who discovered it in 1606.

There is nothing known of Torres's life before and after his great voyage of discovery. He is generally regarded as a Spaniard, almost certainly a Spanish subject; Diego de Prado, an officer who accompanied him on the voyage, said he was a Breton by birth. He is first heard of in July 1605, when he was appointed a commander of one of three vessels under the leadership of Pedro Fernandez de Quiros who was to conduct an expedition in search of *Terra Australis Incognita* — the 'Unknown South Land'. The expedition left Peru from the port of Callao, in December 1605. Torres combined military duties with those of his command; whenever during the voyage to Espiritu Santo (the largest island of the New Hebrides) a landing was made on an island, Quiros put him in charge of the landing party, and in that capacity he was responsible for conducting recurring skirmishes with the natives.

Early in June 1606 Quiros parted company from the expedition at the New Hebrides. Torres, accompanied by Diego de Prado (formerly the senior officer in Quiros's ship), then sailed generally westward, and with difficulty and amid the many dangers of narrow, reef-strewn seas passed between New Guinea and Australia. His farthest point south during the passage appears to have been the southern shore of Banks Island, which he seems to have coasted. Torres arrived in Manila, in the Philippines, by way of the Moluccas, in May 1607.

The evidence for Torres's voyage comprises a letter written by him at Manila, dated July 12, 1607, to Philip III, King of Spain, some other letters and plans of anchorages, and a narrative written later by Prado. A general chart of the voyage, once in existence, is lost.

A special permit from the Queensland Aboriginal Department is necessary to visit some of the islands in the Torres Strait. Yorke Island is one such protected area. In the 1890s it was the home of one of the strangest characters ever known in the North. He was Edward Mosby, a former seaman on an American schooner. Better known as Yankee Ned, he settled down on Yorke and became the self-styled 'king' of the island. He married a handsome and fine type of native woman; four of his sons and several of his grandchildren and great-grandchildren are living on the island.

Yankee Ned gathered a wonderful collection of pearls from the waters surrounding Yorke Island — some of the finest gems ever fished from the Torres Strait. He refused to sell them and few people were privileged to inspect his collection. He told one person they were worth at least £15,000, but, of course, they would be worth very much more today. To safeguard the pearls, Yankee Ned kept them in a glass jar which was placed inside a large clam shell and buried. No one was ever allowed to see where the hoard was buried, and when the owner died he took the secret with him to the grave. Many unsuccessful searches have been made, and although some of the island natives maintain that they know the locality where the pearls were buried they remain undiscovered.

Features of Australian tropical natural history are found in some of the islands of the Torres Strait. Stories of the presence of monkeys in northern Australia, prevalent in the latter years of the last century and the early 1900s, puzzled naturalists until it was shown that the references were to the strange marsupial known as the Cuscus. With its large size, prehensile tail and lemur-like head with small ears, it could justifiably be mistaken for a monkey. Up to half the end of the tail away from the body is covered with scales.

Anatomically the Cuscus is a possum, but so different from all the other possums that it merits a genus, and possibly a sub-family to itself. Though it is confined to the tropics it has a particularly dense coat of fur, generally creamy-white in the females and more or less densely spotted with dark brown in the males. It has the peculiar division of the digits of the hand into two 'thumbs' and three fingers — an adaptation to tree-climbing that is particularly noticeable also in the koala, and to a much less extent in the more familiar possums. The tiny vestige of the external ear is usually hidden beneath the dense fur, so the Cuscus appears to be earless, while its eyes are very large, in correspondence with its nocturnal habits. Slow-moving, the Cuscus sleeps during the day in the forks of trees and eats foliage and native fruits at night. It is also more of a flesh-eater than most other possums, catching birds and small mammals.

The Cuscus is of special zoological interest as it forms a geographical link between the Australian faunal region and the Malayan — it extends with only slight variations from North Queensland through the Torres Strait Islands and New Guinea to Timor and the Celebes on the one hand, and to the Solomon Islands on the other.

51

The Torres Strait Pigeon occurs now in much fewer numbers than formerly throughout its range north of the Tropic of Capricorn. The bird, one of Australia's noblest wild pigeons, has suffered considerably through slaughter; only a few colonies continue to exist on small islands off the Queensland coast. Also called 'nutmeg pigeon', the Torres Strait Pigeon breeds on Woody Island and several other small islets enclosed by the Great Barrier Reef, north of Cardwell, and in Torres Strait itself. The bird's nickname was evidently derived from its fondness for Nutmeg, Quandong, Crinum and other fruits.

Woody Island, main breeding island of the Torres Strait Pigeons, is connected by a coral reef to Low Island, headquarters of the Great Barrier Reef Expedition which spent twelve months there, under the direction of Dr. C. M. Yonge, investigating the formation of coral colonies. Woody Island is about a mile away, to the south-east, and across a lagoon. There these beautiful birds, ivory white, with black flight feathers, build their nests. Each nest contains only a single egg, which is pure lustrous white, and as large as a bantam's. On Woody Island the Torres Strait Pigeons build their nests in mangrove trees, but on some islands with a shortage of nesting space, the nests are built on rocks and the ground, and there are sometimes several in one tree.

Throughout the day, during the nesting season on Woody Island, the birds may be seen arriving with food for their young. The island yields them no food of any kind; the parents are compelled to make extensive journeys to the mainland scrubs, where the fruits they want are obtainable. Flying as much as 50 to 60 miles a day, they travel backwards and forwards past Low Island with its white lighthouse in a pleasing tropical setting of Terminalia trees and palms. The largest flocks are seen just before dusk, when they are hurrying back to the nests before nightfall.

Wonderful navigators, these handsome pigeons are never discouraged by bad weather and never lose their way. A supply-launch owner said that the breeding birds of Woody Island followed a direct course on the sea crossing, and, at times, when through bad visibility he had difficulty in finding Low Island on his fortnightly run with stores for the lighthouse-keepers, he simply steered his boat in the wake of the small groups of pigeons continually appearing out of the mist. With the knowledge that their course would finally bring him to the island, he used the birds for a compass, and they had never let him down.

In spite of statutory protection, numbers of the Torres Strait Pigeon are still destroyed at the breeding grounds, where they are particularly vulnerable. In some instances — such as crews of ships landing to replenish larders — they have been subjected to unrestricted slaughter. The flocks of tremendous size, once so common, are seldom seen now, and only the exercise of greater control over the breeding areas will save the Torres Strait Pigeon from extinction.

7

Prisoners of the Islands

In mid-August, 1834, a raft grounded ashore on Aureed Island, off Cape York. Six men, two women and two children, survivors from the wreck of the barque *Charles Eaton,* trudged wearily ashore. Suddenly a mob of shrieking natives fell on the tragic party. The eight adults were butchered and their heads hacked off as gruesome trophies; yet despite this barbaric slaughter, neither of the children, George D'Oyley, aged seven, and his brother William, aged two, had a finger laid on them by the blood-thirsty natives. A few days later, ship's boy John Ireland and cabin-boy John Sexton, who had survived the same wreck, were brought to the island where they were held in close captivity with the other children for two months.

At the end of this period the natives separated into two parties and left the island. John Sexton and George D'Oyley went with one group and were never heard of again. John Ireland and William D'Oyley, in one of the most remarkable island episodes in Australian history, lived for two years with a tribe of cannibals and head-hunters notorious throughout Cape York Peninsula and the Torres Strait for their savagery.

The *Charles Eaton,* a barque of 313-tons, had sailed from Sydney on a voyage to Sourabaya and Canton with a crew of 23 under the command of Captain Frederick Moore. Her passengers were Dr. Grant, George Armstrong, a London barrister, and Captain D'Oyley of the East India Company's Artillery who was accompanied by his wife, two sons, and an Indian servant woman.

54

Islands north of Cape York, North Queensland

Elcho Island, off Arnhem Land in the Northern Territory

Pearl Divers off the North West coast

When the vessel was well out to sea off Cape Grenville, a heavy storm threatened to rip her canvas to shreds. Captain Moore decided to sail through a narrow channel in the Great Barrier Reef to calmer water. As the ship churned ahead at great speed, the man on the lookout suddenly shouted a warning. Breakers lay dead ahead. The *Charles Eaton* altered course but before she could gather way on the new tack a huge sea caught her broadside and smashed her on a jagged reef off Sir Charles Hardy Island. That submerged reef afterwards became marked 'Detached Reef' on shipping charts. The ship was held fast and there was no immediate danger unless the weather worsened. Unluckily the gale increased in force, and when the captain ordered the long-boat to be launched to investigate how much buffeting the hulk would stand, a giant wave smashed it to splinters against the coral. During a momentary calm a smaller cutter was launched, manned by seaman James Price. Tragedy struck again when another hissing green mountain of water bore down crushing man and boat in the coral-studded sea; neither was seen again.

Only one boat, a cutter capable of holding no more than eight persons, remained. George Piggott, the bosun, Laurance Constantine, a carpenter, and a seaman quickly lowered it and the three of them pushed clear of the wreck. As it began to move away, two other seamen leapt from the slowly disintegrating hull, swam to the boat and were dragged aboard. Then the five deserters pulled away, leaving passengers and the rest of the crew marooned on the doomed barque.

All through that night those on the wreck suffered agonies of mind wondering whether they would live to see the next day, but dawn broke on a clear sky and calm waters. With a measure of hope the men began to build a raft from loose timbers on the vessel. When finished, and the sun shining, the raft was launched and found to float well. Mrs D'Oyley and her two boys together with the Bengalese woman servant were first placed on it, followed by some of the men. A second raft was found necessary to hold the rest of the ship's company, and while this was being built, the first one paddled off.

After a perilous voyage this first raft finally grounded to rest on Aureed Island, where they were attacked by the head-hunters and only the lives of two-years-old William D'Oyley and his seven-years-old brother, George, were spared. The second raft drifted for seven days, the castaways existing on a daily ration of two draughts of water and half a ship's biscuit. When they reached the island of Boydong, about 40 miles north-west of the wreck, they, too, were attacked by natives and all were massacred except the two boys John Ireland and John Sexton. Soon after, the boys were taken by canoe to Aureed Island where they joined the two other young survivors.

The natives on Aureed came from different islands. After a lot of haggling among the chiefs, when the time came for their return to their islands the four boy prisoners were divided. One party took George D'Oyley and George Sexton, never to be heard of or seen again, while John Ireland and William D'Oyley were taken to Marsden Island where they were well treated and kept as curiosities. Natives from all parts of the Torres Strait visited Marsden Island to look at the strange white children who had come out of the sea. It was believed that they were reincarnations of deceased natives.

Among the visitors was a chief named Duppah who also brought his wife with him. They took such a fancy to the boys that the chief bought them for two bunches of bananas. Duppah then carried off his prizes to his home on Mer, now called Murray Island. One day the trading vessel *Mangles*, under the command of Captain William Carr, anchored off Mer Island. Among the natives who came out in canoes to trade was John Ireland. He told the captain the tragic story of the wreck of the *Charles Eaton*, but when he was offered a chance to escape he was reluctant, saying that he was happy enough and contented. Next day Captain Carr landed on the island to investigate the story and, sure enough, saw the young boy William D'Oyley whom the natives made no attempt to hide.

When Captain Carr eventually returned to Sydney and revealed the news of the two young castaways on Mer Island, Governor Bourke took action. As a result the colonial cutter *Isabella,* under the command of Captain Lewis, left Sydney for Torres Strait in May 1836. It was nearly two years after the wreck that the *Isabella* reached Mer Island. This time John Ireland decided to return to civilization, and the chief, Duppah, did not mind parting with him. Duppah boarded the *Isabella,* quite ready to trade the white youth for a bright new hatchet. He was unwilling, however, to hand over William D'Oyley who had become a great favourite of his wife and himself, and, indeed, the pet of all the islanders. Eventually, but with great reluctance, Duppah agreed to surrender the boy in exchange for another tomahawk. But young Will D'Oyley cried bitterly when taken from his native foster mother. When he was rescued the boy had no knowledge of English, but he could speak the native island language fluently for a child of four.

Captain Lewis' task was also to get proof of the wreck and to account as far as possible for all the ship's company. On leaving Murray (Mer) Island with the two young survivors he visited Aureed Island. Ireland's memory of the tragic events enabled Lewis to find a hideous memento of the slaughter on Aureed Island. It was a huge turtle shell painted to resemble a mask, and around the edge of it were a number of skulls tied with rope of European origin. The skulls were identified as those of white people, with the hair still attached. Judging from the long locks of one it was the skull of a woman, and the comb which was still in the hair suggested strongly that it was all that remained of Mrs. D'Oyley. The skulls were brought back to Sydney and were finally buried in the cemetery at Bunnerong. Today, a headstone over the grave records that under it are interred the skulls brought back from the Torres Strait island by Captain Lewis of the *Isabella.* The comb which adorned the hair of the female skull is — at least it was until recent years — in the possession of a Queenslander.

Governor Bourke rewarded Captain Lewis for his part in the rescue by appointing him harbour-master at Port

Phillip, Victoria. Young Will D'Oyley was taken into the household of a Mrs Anne Slade in Sydney, but later Lewis took the youngster to England and placed him in the care of his father's family. There he grew up to follow his father's profession in the service of the East India Company. John Ireland settled down to a job ashore and never returned to the sea.

As to the five deserters from the wreck of the *Charles Eaton*. They sailed through Torres Strait, and one man died before the rest reached Timor-Laut. From there they made their way to Amboyna where they told their story, colouring it to justify their desertion. In due course a trading vessel took them to England where they were able to add further information on the loss of the *Charles Eaton*.

With the return of young D'Oyley and Ireland, some people were not satisfied that the teenagers Sexton and George D'Oyley were dead, and as a result of persistent agitation Captain Thomas Watson sailed from Sydney for further searches. Watson called first at Murray Island where he presented lavish and numerous presents to Duppah and his wife who had befriended Will D'Oyley and John Ireland. Duppah could throw no light on the fate of the two missing youths but he brought along a chief named Oby who told Watson that there was a white man being held captive by the natives of Timor-Laut. It was this information that eventually led to the rescue of the former cabin-boy Joseph Forbes, and the solving of the mystery of the missing schooner *Stedcombe*.

The documented story of Joseph Forbes will be found in the *Transactions of the Historical Society of Australasia* in the form of a paper read before the Society in September 1886 by Admiral Pascoe, who possessed the journal of Captain Watson, the rescuer of Forbes.

The year was 1823 when the 15-year-old cabin boy Joseph Forbes sailed from Melville Island, North Australia, aboard the schooner *Stedcombe* to get livestock for the garrison at Fort Dundas. The mate had a crew of 12 seamen and two cabin boys, Forbes and John Edwards, when they made for the nearest Indonesian island — Timor-Laut. As soon as the schooner moored, the mate and crew rowed to the shore leaving on board the steward and the two cabin boys.

The boy Joseph Forbes was watching the ship's party through a telescope as they landed on the beach when suddenly he saw a scene that nearly froze his blood in horror. At a signal from the islanders who welcomed them ashore, the men were attacked. Outnumbered twenty to one, it was only a matter of moments before the twelve English sailors were trussed on the beach like turkeys. The boy's horror turned to terror when he saw the natives with their razor-edged knives neatly sever the heads of all their helpless victims.

As he shouted to the other cabin boy and the steward, a canoe came rapidly towards the *Stedcombe*. In a matter of moments it was alongside and savage islanders were climbing aboard. One, seizing an axe, cut off the steward's head. After the schooner had been plundered it was set on fire and the two cabin-boys were taken ashore as slaves. When within a few months the second boy pined away and died, Joe Forbes was in a more miserable state than ever; a white boy alone among savages.

Every day he was forced to work in the rice fields and to clear land of timber, and at night he was locked up in a hut. Whenever a ship appeared, the natives bound and gagged the youth and hid him in a secret cave. Gradually he forgot the English language and spoke only the native one. Such was Joe Forbes' life for sixteen long years. As nothing could be traced concerning the ill-fated *Stedcombe*, since she left Melville Island, it was thought that she must have foundered during a storm or cyclone — just another mystery of the South Seas.

When Captain Watson set sail for Timor-Laut in the schooner *Essington* to investigate the report of a captive white man he was advised that a Dutch skipper had also reported rumours of the captive. Watson arrived at his destination on March 31, 1839. He had a good knowledge of the Malayan language and announced to the natives there that he had many trading goods on display; by this means he was able to coax the chief of the island to board

59

the ship. Producing a pair of brightly polished handcuffs, he told the chief that they were ankle ornaments, and to demonstrate he locked one handcuff around the leg of the chief and then immediately locked the other on to a deck-bolt.

At the same time the members of the crew made their appearance armed with guns. Though trapped, the chief denied that there was any white man on his island, but when a looped rope was slipped over his neck he knew that the skipper meant business. He signalled his warriors ashore to send at once to the ship a canoe with the white prisoner.

Eventually a canoe came out from the beach paddling full speed with a strange-looking passenger on board. His golden hair had not been cut for sixteen years, and his body, naked except for a brief loin-cloth, was covered with scars and ulcers. 'There's your Christian slave!' said the pinioned Malay chief. 'Now keep your word and let me go!'

Skipper Tom Watson kept his word, and kicked the chief off the schooner as soon as the rescued Christian was on board. Alas, the long-haired slave, through lack of practice, had almost forgotten how to speak English. Captain Watson, in his journal, describes the rescued man in these words:

'The appearance of this Englishman at the time we received him on board drew forth the strongest sympathies from all of us. He appeared to be less than thirty years old, of a remarkably fair complexion notwithstanding the effects of a tropical climate. His hair which was of a light yellow colour was about twenty inches long, and its texture very much resembled fine silk in its raw state. It was triced up after the native custom with a bamboo comb.

'His only garment was a loin-cloth. There was a peculiar vacancy in his expression and there was a marked look of agony in his face which, no doubt, from long suffering had become habitual. His body was much emaciated and covered with scars, and the sinews about the knee-joints were so much contracted as to prevent him from being able to work. His ears had been perforated with large holes through which were threaded pieces of bamboo of at least an inch in diameter. It was only with difficulty that he could make himself intelligible, for he had practically forgotten his English language.'

After listening carefully to the sailors' talk for a few days the long-haired Joseph regained the use of his mother-tongue and joined in a shanty or two. Rapidly then his rusty tongue was unloosed and he was able to tell the terrible tale of his adventures with the Malays. Nicknamed 'Timor Joe', on the journey back to Australia he made a remarkable recovery of his health and spirits.

One day he said to Captain Watson: 'I have no money to pay you for saving me so I will give you my hair.' There and then he snipped off his twenty-inch-long golden tresses of silken texture and presented them to his saviour.

On his arrival in Sydney, Timor Joe became a celebrity. He was given a trip to London where he had the honour of being presented to Queen Victoria — to whom he told the story of his capture and slavery, omitting only those parts which were not fit for Her Majesty's ear. On his return to Australia he settled at Williamstown, near Melbourne, where he earned his livelihood as a fisherman. His golden locks were preserved as a curio by the Watson family in Sydney.

There have been several instances of white youths being given kindly treatment by the same natives who massacred adults, white or otherwise. The French cabin-boy Narcisse Pierre Pellatier who became a tribesman was another example. He was aboard the ship *St. Paul* carrying a passenger list of 350 Chinese immigrants for Australia when the vessel hit a rock off a nameless island in northern waters. The captain and crew took to the available ship's boats, cast away with them and, on the ground of insufficient space, left the Chinese and the cabin-boy to their fate — a shocking one in the case of the Chinese. These were retained by a neighbouring cannibal tribe, who ate them off systematically, fattening them while holding them prisoners. Sixteen of the three hundred and fifty Chinese were rescued in the course of time, and lived to tell the gory tale.

The fate of the crew is uncertain; there was a story that

61

they reached New Caledonia, but it seems unlikely that such a long journey could be successfully negotiated in open boats with scanty provisions. Narcisse was adopted by Queensland natives, becoming in a matter of months a formal member of the Makadama tribe and in a matter of years a true tribal warrior. He went naked with them in the bush, hunting and fishing, and occasionally fighting a neighbouring tribe. His body became a gleaming copper colour, and his chest scarified by the formal ceremonies of manhood. A piece of wood, four inches long, pierced the lobe of his ear.

The most interesting part about Pellatier is that he resisted degradation. While he learnt the language of his adopted people, he did not forget his own. His education had been rudimentary at the time of his entry into primitive life, but it did not regress or even stay at the same level; it improved. He improved his counting and mastery of numbers, and became a proficient artist and draftsman, drawing and recording many of the new wonders he found in animal and botanical life.

His memory of the past faded after the years passed by, and he came to regard himself fully and completely as a member of the tribe. How he retained his capacity for reading is a mystery, unless he kept it by constant writing; but with what instruments except a piece of wood on the sand, or with clay on bark, is unknown, if indeed there were any. The former cabin-boy lived with the tribe of savages for 17 years, and those years the most formative of any man's life.

On April 11, 1875, he was discovered, by whom is not recorded, though at that time there were many pioneering parties operating by sea and land in the task of pushing the frontier back. Recognised as a white man, they claimed him for their own. He did not want to leave his tribe, nor did the tribe want him to go. It took a lot of persuasion to get him away, and it is an interesting commentary on his innate common sense that he did consent to go; for he had never turned his back on civilization, and this fateful choice had to be made.

Taking his sketches, of which he had hundreds — all of them of inestimable scientific value — and his memories, he put on some clothing again, bade goodbye to his black brothers, and within a few months was back among his people in Bordeaux, France. It has been claimed that Pellatier returned from France to live with the aborigines who had befriended him, and that he died in their midst when an old man in 1924.

One of the few instances of a white woman being taken by savage islanders and given privileged treatment concerns the young Scotswoman, Barbara Thompson. Brought to New South Wales by her parents in the late 1830s, she married at the age of sixteen and was with her husband in the cutter *America* when it was driven by a gale on to a reef at Possession Island. The storm lasted for two days and nights during which two of the crew were washed overboard and drowned. The remaining two seamen, Mrs Thompson, and her husband lashed themselves to the deck. On the third morning the storm abated and they found they had drifted to another island. While they were wondering about its location, a fleet of canoes packed with natives put off from the shore and soon the drifting boat was surrounded by a yelling horde of savages. They clambered on board, and although Mrs Thompson's husband tried hard to make friends with them it was useless. They killed him, and killed also the other two men. Barbara Thompson was taken prisoner.

The story of the white lubra was first learned when H.M.S. *Rattlesnake,* an Admiralty surveying vessel from Sydney, was in the waters of Torres Strait. On October 16, 1848, Able Seaman Scott with a landing party from the ship came ashore at Evans' Bay, Cape York. He had orders to obtain birds and animals for scientific purposes and he brushed aside the natives who clustered around the sailors. Most of the natives gave way as the boat's crew moved across the sands, but a lubra stood almost directly in their path. Scott ignored her and walked quickly past, when the lubra stumbled forward a few feet and cried in a broken voice:

'I am a white woman! Why do you leave me?'

The startled sailor turned and looked at the woman. She wore only an apron of fibre; she was dirty, her skin was tanned and blistered, one eye was closed. But she was unquestionably a white woman. Scott stared, open-mouthed, bewildered, and when the boat's crew began to crowd around her the woman burst into tears. She was given two of the sailors' shirts, one of which she wore in the normal style, the other wrapped around her waist as a skirt, and then she was led down to the beach and rowed out to the *Rattlesnake*.

In the captain's cabin the white woman told her story haltingly in a mixture of English and native words. Captain Owen Stanley, R.N., half-suspecting that she might be an escaped convict from the Moreton Bay penal settlement, asked her gently if she was sure she wanted to be taken back to civilization. (The penalty for runaway convicts was generally death.) The young woman, however, assured him that her story was true.

She had lived for about four and a half years mostly on Prince Edward Island, having been taken prisoner on Possession Island. One of the tribal elders, Piaguai, decided that Barbara was the reincarnation of his dead daughter Giaom. He formally adopted her as his daughter and she soon found herself a full member of the tribe. From the start, her supernatural origin gave her a specially privileged place in the tribe and she was not expected to work like the other lubras. When the women went out digging yams and carrying heavy loads she remained in the camps minding the babies. The men treated her with respect but the women resented this pampered newcomer, although they dare not show their jealousy openly.

Despite privileged treatment Barbara Thompson suffered many hardships. She lost the sight of one eye through contracting an eye disease, and her body was covered with old burn scars through sleeping too close to the fire on cold nights. During her captivity on the island she had occasionally seen ships far out at sea; none had come close enough for her to attract attention. When she learned by native smoke signal that a ship was in Evans Bay she had persuaded three of her tribal 'brothers' to take her to visit the ship in order to obtain axes, knives and tobacco. The natives had done so, convinced that no one would willingly give up privileged conditions such as she held.

From the day that Barbara boarded the *Rattlesnake* she never left the workroom which Captain Stanley gave her as a cabin. Even when the *Rattlesnake* cruised leisurely about the tropical islands and New Guinea — its whole voyage lasted four years — she was too terrified to go ashore. When at length the *Rattlesnake* arrived back in Sydney, Barbara Thompson was able to give authorities much useful information about the natives including words and grammar of the Muralug, the tribe with whom she lived.

One of the most remarkable stories Mrs Thompson had to tell concerned a mysterious white man who reigned as 'king' on Badu, a nearby island to that on which she was held captive. She said that about a year after she had been taken prisoner her chieftain 'father' received a command from this white man to bring her over to his island of Badu. The chief dare not refuse for fear that his tribe would be wiped out by the native followers of the White Devil.

Strangely enough, the white man — a Frenchman — received her with the greatest courtesy. Then he started to boast of his powers, describing how he had trained his savages to kill every white man they saw, to attack every boat that neared his island. The natives carried out his orders to the letter. They were terrified of him and looked upon him as a kind of living devil — which in truth he was.

Mrs Thompson said that she was convinced the Frenchman was a madman, and added that while he was talking to her he suddenly flew into a violent rage and ordered the chief to take her back. She never saw this extraordinary man again.

On hearing her story the Queensland Police Department decided to investigate. They sent a small expedition by launch to Badu Island. Sure enough, as they drew near, a fleet of canoes full of armed natives came out to attack them. But the police were ready, and seizing their rifles they picked off the steersman of each canoe. This caused panic among the natives, and they put back to the island.

The Frenchman met them on the beach, raging at them in his mad fury and cursing them for their cowardice. He tried to rally them to attack, but it was useless; they fled headlong into the bush. This was too much for their white chief. Seizing a club he sprang at his own men, killing several before they had time to escape. Very soon he was left alone on the beach.

As the police put in and waded ashore the Frenchman turned on them. Frothing at the mouth, and with his eyes blazing fearfully, he presented a terrible sight as he rushed towards the new arrivals. He held aloft a spear; his body had been burnt black by the sun and was decorated with necklaces of sharks' teeth. Around his loins was the skin of a shark, and he wore a magnificent headdress of Bird-of-Paradise feathers. When the madman halted to hurl his spear at the nearest man, a shot rang out, and without a sound the Frenchman fell dead. So ended the White Devil of Badu.

A strange instance of a white woman's association with the aborigines is told by Lady Broome in her *Colonial Memories,* published in 1904. About 1885-1886, two or three years after her husband Sir Frederick Broome had become Governor of Western Australia, Lady Broome accompanied him to the post-office to receive the first message over a new telegraph-line to an outpost in the Kimberleys.

The trooper sergeant at the outpost sent a message stating that there was a native tribe in the district with a white woman and her son living with them. The woman and her son (then a baby) had been on a vessel wrecked 20 years before — in the 1860s — and had lived with the aborigines ever since. The woman still spoke English and she told the sergeant that she and her son had been well treated by the natives. They had shown her every consideration, and when her feet were sore from going bare-footed they would always wait for her. The sergeant added that she had blue eyes but was tanned almost as dark as the natives, who looked upon her as a kind of queen.

Intrigued with this message, the vice-regal couple telegraphed another one inviting the woman to return to civilization. Back came the reply stating that she declined with thanks as she and her son were happy with the natives. She also said that there was nothing either of them required, but if the Governor and his lady cared they could send some blankets and a little flour for the natives. These were later despatched together with a supply of tea. The subsequent history of the woman and her son is unknown.

8

The Pearling Centre

MOST Australians are familiar with the name of Thursday Island, yet very few of them have visited this top-of-the-map outpost. Southerners — the bulk of Australia's population — seeking an island holiday away from it all have tropical islands much nearer home, and probably feel that Thursday would scarcely warrant the long journey necessary to reach there. True, it has much in common with other tropical islands — it has its golden sands, rustling palms, eternal sunshine, and crystal-clear waters that make swimming and fishing a perpetual delight. But it has much more than that. Thursday Island is intriguing — a happy hunting ground for unusual facets of Australiana. Moreover, the island is not a tourist one and the visitor is welcomed as a person rather than a potential customer.

Perched like one of its own pearls on the forehead of Australia, the island has been called the pearly gateway to New Guinea, from which it is separated by only 80 miles. Thursday is important as the pearling centre, principal port of call, and quarantine and customs station of the Torres Strait area. It is also the headquarters of Barrier Reef pilots. There are regular services by air and sea; the former being three times weekly while the boat calls once every four weeks.

Travelling by air from the southern cities, the plane journey terminates at Horn Island, four miles across the sea from Thursday Island which is too small and hilly for aircraft landings. Horn Island is splendidly suitable with a first-rate drome and many bitumen strips. This is a legacy from the U.S. Air Force base for Superfortresses before the battle for the Coral Sea. Journey's end on this wide, flat island, brings out a new atmosphere with the sleek, copper-skinned Torres Strait Islanders appearing on the tarmac ready to unload the plane. But it is over on Thursday Island where there is always a friendly group of people waiting to greet new arrivals that you find the traditional atmosphere of the South Seas. Though Thursday Island lacks the sophistication of tropical centres such as Singapore, Panama and Colombo, the waterfront seems like a typical Somerset Maugham stage setting with the frangipani and leaning coconut palms, catamarans and assorted sailing vessels, and all drenched in dazzling sunshine. A pleasant surprise is the almost non-existence of flies and mosquitoes.

The native people are a racial mosaic: Torres Strait Islanders, half-castes, Malays, Cingalese, Indonesians, Filipinos, Chinese and South Sea Islanders. There are also Australian-born Japanese as well as the imported Japanese pearl divers. As is found in nearly every community in the world, there is the inevitable Chinese trader. Of fine physique and intelligent, the dusty-brown islanders are likeable and friendly, rarely without a smile. They take pride in their homes and jobs, and in their native mat and craft ware. Like their forefathers they delight in feasting and dancing on special occasions. A problem with these native people is illegitimacy, arising mainly from their fervent love of babies. Such children are never unwanted; extra mouths to feed make little difference on an island where nobody need go hungry. With coconuts and oysters abounding, you just pick them up and eat them whenever you feel like it. The fish (and their size and variety are astonishing) bite so well that any tyro, man or woman, can pull up two at a time.

Romance descended on Thursday Island with pearl fishing. The island's traders export pearl and trochus shell, beche-de-mer and pearls. Trochus shells are shaped like cones and have spiral patterns. They are heavily coated with a lime formation which is removed with acid, after which the shells are burnished. Then they look like pearl shells and are used for making buttons. A residue is used for making face powder. The two square miles of Thursday Island have exported trochus shell to many countries. Australians there don't care for this shell fish for eating, but the natives make a delicious soup with it. China buys large quantities of smoked trochus to delight its epicures. Beche-de-mer, a kind of sea-cucumber, is also relished by the Chinese palate.

Unfortunately for this island of the pearl fishers, a formidable competitor has lately appeared — the plastic pearl button. As a result there has been a considerable drop in the pearl shell market, and the many islanders who work in the industry are not as busy as they might be. Nevertheless the men behind the pearl shell management are pinning their hopes on a new venture — the culture of pearl shell. Experiments have shown that pearls cultured here in the Torres Strait are better than those grown in Japan, the home of that technique. There is no mother-of-pearl shell in Japanese waters and all pearls grown in Japan are cultured in Akoya shell. Japanese experts are working in conjunction with an Australian company at Thursday Island and finding that the local shell is giving remarkably successful results in pearl culture.

Trochus divers can easily be distinguished from pearl divers by the colour of their hair. The trochus men spend more time around the surface of the sunlit tropic waters and their black fuzzy hair has a golden tan colour on top, much admired by the invariably vain natives. It is a general belief that the men use peroxide of hydrogen for bleaching their hair to obtain the desired shade, but the natives deny this. No self-respecting male, however, would go about his business without his hand mirror and comb.

All the Torres Strait pearling crews are highly superstitious. Under no circumstances will they leave port on a Friday or set sail with a crew of thirteen. If it is impossible to obtain an additional member to that unlucky number, either one man must drop out or an animal — even a bird — taken on board to make up fourteen souls. Generally seventeen islanders form the crew of a trochus lugger.

Great Palm Island, off the Queensland coast

*South Molle Island, with Mid Molle and North Molle,
in the Whitsunday Group*

Sunset on Orpheus Island, Queensland

While still only a youngster, the Torres Strait Islander has learned the rudiments of pearling and the dangers of the deep. He knows of the terrifying strength of the giant clam and the deadliness of the groper with its ability to swallow a human body whole. Trochus shell divers do not use any artificial breathing apparatus. The pearl diver uses a weighted helmet over his head, otherwise the rest of his body is uncovered.

Every Christmas when the pearling season has come to an end and the luggers return to their home port at Thursday Island, natives gather from all over the island to begin the 'welcome home' party — a gay round of festivities that may last several weeks.

The pearling luggers have made these islands famous. With wonderful sea-keeping qualities, they stand up to the fiercest weather when on their quest for the sea-bed's wealth. The Queensland Protector of Islanders cares for the natives and the luggers which are all manned by the islanders. All know the pearling beds well, but the objects of their searches are often gained at costly price, the cemeteries emphasizing the hazards risked by divers who braved the sharks and other dangers once too often. The Japanese are splendid divers, partly because of their physique and partly because of their peculiarly fatalistic minds. The native is a capable diver, too.

The island cemetery comprises three burial grounds, European, Japanese and aboriginal. On many of the Japanese graves are perched small cement bird-cages containing food for the spirits of departed divers. As well as food, they sometimes contain tins of tobacco, boxes of matches and bottles of beer. A festive touch is occasionally added with the addition of flags and bunting.

The white population numbers about 500, while the native population, who are always referred to as islanders, comprises some 800. The T.I.'s — as the white residents refer to themselves — have such a deep affection for their island that they have a club in Brisbane where former residents meet regularly, reminiscing nostalgically of their halcyon days up North. Among those who have made

71

permanent homes on T.I. are the 'Island Queen', Mrs McNulty, who was the first white woman born there, 88-year-old Arthur Sullivan and Frank Robertson, two of the best-known of the 'pearling kings'. These and other old-timers like to yarn of the strange happenings and the odd characters of the past, of the days when the island boasted the world's smallest daily newspaper. Known as the *Torres Strait Daily Pilot,* it was founded by a woman in 1888. The unique sheet was sought by collectors of curios all over the world.

A favourite story concerns the letter posted on the island and addressed to Normanton in Queensland which cost no less than £166.3.4 to deliver. The Postmaster-General's department had leased the mail contract for deliveries from Thursday Island to Queensland at £2,000 per annum. In the first month of this service being opened only one letter was mailed by any of Thursday Island's residents; hence it was a costly letter for the Department.

Until recent years, Treacle, a Torres Strait Islander, was a living attraction for Thursday Island visitors, because he lived to tell the tale after having been literally half engulfed by a giant groper. In support of his story he wore a souvenir necklace in the form of a circle of livid scars covering his thorax. He compelled the great groper to disgorge its troublesome morsel by gouging out its eyes with his thumbs. The toughness of the Treacle topknot was attested to by the removal by Dr. W. Verno of Thursday Island hospital of several of the groper's teeth which had become firmly embedded in the native's skull.

A stranger case, perhaps, is that of the Thursday Island native who was horribly mauled by a shark when pearl diving. His mates thought him dead and sewed him up in canvas on the lugger for burial. So firm was the sewing that the shroud acted as a ligature, staunching the copious flow, and when he was about to be buried the canvas cocoon was seen to move. He returned to pearl diving.

It is a very moving sight to see the luggers come into Thursday Island when there has been the death of a native diver. The dead man's brightly coloured lava-lava is flown at half-mast from that part of the lugger where he last dived. As the vessel comes into port all the other luggers in the vicinity — maybe a fleet of twenty — fall into line and follow the cortège to the Thursday Island jetty.

To reach the island by ship, vessels steam through the Prince of Wales Channel where they are likely to meet with a tidal stream of seven knots. That makes the ship travel either like a speedboat or a tortoise, according to whether it is flood tide or ebb. Before the pilot comes to take the ship into port, he notes the direction in which the tide is setting at the wharf. As the ship passes close to Vivien Point, the township of Port Kennedy opens up, and the pilot watches to see if a man on the wharf waves a flag to let him know if the tide's direction has changed. Nobody has yet succeeded in calculating the tide's activities around T.I., although one man spent a year trying to before giving up the maddening task.

Walking along the defence road you could go round the island in an hour. The Queensland Government maintains various officials there, but natives have a say in their government too. Three native councillors elected by their fellows wear panama hats and bright red jerseys with the word COUNCILLOR in white letters across their chests.

Fronted by a large lawn and surrounded by bougainvillea, frangipani and tall palms, stands the All Souls' Quetta Memorial Cathedral, the walls of which embody a stone from England's Canterbury Cathedral. Erected in remembrance of the victims of Australia's worst coastal shipping disaster, parts of the wrecked *Quetta* have been put to practical use in the beautiful stone church and are constant reminders to worshippers of the tragedy. The ship's bell is rung for the daily office; the compass has been made into one of the fonts; a copper jug is used as a ewer at the baptismal font; the teak slab from the ship's wheelbox now forms the top of the credence in the chapel. Above the high altar is suspended as a perpetually burning sanctuary lamp, the former riding light of the *Quetta*; the lectern is made from timber from the wreck. A porthole covered with eighteen years' growth of coral, a lifebuoy and a flag also have their place among the relics. Many of the stained-glass windows in the cathedral were placed there in memory of ones who lost their lives in the wreck.

The *Quetta*, a fine, trim ship, was one of the latest passenger steamers on the London-Brisbane run and was regarded as safe and seaworthy as any to be found on the seven seas. When she departed from the Brisbane wharf in February 1890 her passengers had a gay send-off from friends which was slightly marred by the ship's stern grazing a shed on the edge of the wharf, tearing off yards of planking with a splintering crash. However, she soon righted herself with the drag of the tug's hawsers and, without further incident, steamed off. Nevertheless, superstitious members of the crew regarded the bad start as an ominous sign.

It was a smooth and uneventful voyage all along the North Australian coast until the evening of February 28, 1890, when the *Quetta* was travelling through Adolphus Channel in Torres Strait at 13 knots. It was a night of radiant moonlight with the sea exceptionally calm, and many of the passengers were strolling along the decks admiring the beauty of the tropical seascape. Captain Saunders was on the bridge with the pilot, who was taking the ship through the channel. He knew every rock and shoal and there was little need for him to consult the Admiralty charts, so carefully plotted over years of oceanic survey.

A few minutes after the ship's bell rang 9 o'clock the *Quetta* struck something with a grinding crash that made the vessel shudder from stem to stern. She floundered off course as the engines stopped. It was thought that the *Quetta* had collided with a derelict but seconds later the stunned captain realized that the impossible had happened; the vessel had struck an uncharted rock.

He shouted to the chief officer to launch the boats as the *Quetta* heeled over to port at a sickening angle. Water was pouring into the ship through the huge rent the rock had sheared in her side, trapping the engine-room crew and firemen. Bewildered and frantic passengers clung to the rails as Captain Saunders strove with his officers to get the women and children first into the boats. But the panic-stricken lascar crew and some Javanese passengers frustrated their efforts and in a frenzy of fear rushed the boats trampling down and thrusting aside all who opposed them.

The British officers fought them with their fists and drew their revolvers, but the lascars managed to get away in the first two boats, one of which was swamped with its weight of numbers, and the occupants flung into the water. Most of the women and children were able to be accommodated in the remaining boats before the *Quetta* took her final plunge.

There were many tragic happenings on that dreadful night, and of the 282 people aboard the *Quetta* only 109 were saved. The heavy loss of life was primarily due to the fact that the coloured crew became unmanageable. Surviving passengers described how screaming lascars had seized them in the water and scrambled into one of the boats with women and children until their numbers caused it to overturn.

The mystery of the uncharted rock was solved when survey vessels later found that it was a pinnacle of growing coral which had built up over the thirty-odd years since the earlier surveys had been made.

One of the three female survivors of the wreck, Mrs Alice Horsley, died in Brisbane in November, 1951, at the age of 81. Another was the late Mrs Cecil McDonald, of Southport, Queensland. She was a baby when the *Quetta* went to her doom. Survivors who saw the child when she was taken from the water could not identify her, and Captain Brown, the Torres Strait pilot, adopted her and she grew up under the name of Quetta Brown. She afterwards married a relative of the captain.

Quetta relics and other reminders of lost ships may be seen in the Thursday Island museum. One is a bell that apparently served two masters. It was found on a Torres Strait island many years ago; one side of the bell bears the inscription 'Ship *Sally*, 1807', and the other side is inscribed 'Schooner *Triumph*, 1847'. Neither of these two ships has been identified — it is thought the bell came off a 'blackbirding' vessel. Alongside it is another bell from a lost ship, one that is believed to have come from the 'black-birding' craft called the *Young Dick*. That vessel was exploiting Kanaka labour in the islands for the Queensland sugar plantations in 1886 when she suddenly disappeared in a storm off the Queensland coast. Wreckage was picked up later near Hinchinbrook Island, where she had last been seen; but nothing was heard of the 150 Kanakas and crew of 30 she had on board. Years afterwards, this ship's bell was found on the reefs in the vicinity by a pearling lugger.

Behind the cathedral rises Green Hill, thickly covered with shrubs and trees. A closer look discloses the bricks and stones of battlements now weathered and overgrown. The fortified hill, which was given the name of Battery Point last century, is honeycombed with deeply-built storehouses. Ancient five-ton, three-inch guns lie rusting in the tangled vines and undergrowth. Interesting, too, are the decaying relics of the golden days when the same hill gave up gold to the pans of hopeful miners.

Thursday Island — its native name is Wai-ben — with other islands lying within 60 miles of the coast of Queensland, was annexed to that colony in 1872. It is not certain who named Thursday Island, but the general belief is that Captain Cook was responsible. Sunday and Wednesday Islands were named by Captain Bligh in 1792, but Thursday Island does not appear in any publication before an Admiralty chart of 1850. European settlement dates from 1877, when the coaling station and port formerly established at Somerset on the mainland was transferred to Port Kennedy.

It was on nearby Possession Island, an insignificant spot three and a half square miles in area, whose name most Australians have never heard, where Australia became British territory. It was here that Cook made the comprehensive and formal proclamation in which the island-continent came to the realm of the British king. Set on a rock overlooking a beach on Possession Island is a simple concrete memorial fashioned with sand from the shore where Cook and his party pulled in their boats. Its inscription reads:
Captain James Cook, R.N., of the *Endeavour*, landed

on this island, which he named Possession Island, and in the name of His Majesty King George III took possession of the whole of the eastern coast of Australia from latitude of 38 degrees south to this place. August 22nd, 1770.'

Had Cook known that gold lay beneath his feet when he landed on Possession Island the development of Australia would probably have taken a different course. Within a few feet of the spot where Cook planted his flagstaff, the explorer and surveyor J. T. Embley discovered gold in 1895. There he sank a shaft (it is still to be seen) and with a group of others worked it for several years. 2,480 ounces of pure gold were taken from Possession Island, and from neighbouring Horn Island, where gold had been located in 1894, some 1,081 ounces were obtained.

There are four hotels on Thursday Island, a Chamber of Commerce, a Country Women's Association and several lodges. Unconventional dress is noticeable and the hotel bars seem to be always crowded. Still, the churches have good attendances (there are three, also a convent) and congregations are looked after by six clergymen. Of the three schools, one is entirely aboriginal. A warm friendliness between all sections of the community is most apparent on this lovely island of great potential. Whether this potential will be fully developed is problematical for like most tropical islands things have a habit of drifting on a sea of apathy, encouraged, no doubt, by the drowsing days of endless summer.

9

The Blackbirders

THE islands of North Queensland and the Torres Strait saw many a 'blackbirding' vessel with its human cargo bound for the mainland of Queensland and northern New South Wales. Between 1847 and 1904 approximately 57,000 natives from the Solomon Islands, the New Hebrides, the islands of New Guinea and the Torres Strait were taken from their homes often in circumstances of brutality, violence and deception. Generally known by the Polynesian name of kanakas, their introduction was to supply cheap labour for the sugar plantations and cotton fields of the North. Kanakas were also used for pearl-diving in Torres Strait.

The story of the kanakas is a sorry tale of abuse and often tragedy which has largely been forgotten. The blackbirders raided villages, captured the islanders at sea in their canoes, or maybe enticed them aboard the luggers with gifts of tobacco and trinkets. They would be battened down in the hold to be sorted out — the old and the very young natives tossed overboard — on the way to the mainland. In theory, the islanders were engaged of their own free will for a term of three years, 'recruited' by the skippers of luggers and supposedly under 'contract'. Instead, they were brought to this country virtually as slaves.

Commander A. H. Markham, R.N., reporting on blackbirding activities in February 1872, said that a nefarious system of kidnapping was practised 'to an almost inconceivable extent'. It amounted, he said, to slavery; in many cases, to murder. Even twenty years earlier official circles

78

were made aware of the many abuses in the trade. Earl Grey, the Colonial Secretary, wrote to Governor Fitzroy referring to reports of outrages committed by labour recruiters and expressing the anxious desire of the Government that natives should not be ill-treated by British subjects.

Robert Towns, after whom Townsville was named, was one of the first to introduce kanakas for labouring. Some of their descendants can be found working as fishermen or on cane farms in Queensland and the Tweed River district of New South Wales. Indeed, there are still a very few old kanakas in Australia who in their youth were clubbed into insensibility on island beaches and dragged aboard blackbirding luggers for this shocking trade.

Henry Lewin, one of many blackbirders who scoured the islands for cheap labour and made a fortune out of the infamous business, put the following advertisement in a Brisbane newspaper of April 26, 1867:

SUGAR PLANTERS, COTTON GROWERS, AND OTHERS.

Henry Ross Lewin, for many years engaged in trade in the South Sea Islands, and well acquainted with the language and habits of the natives, begs to inform the public that he will be happy to receive orders for the importation of South Sea natives. For the past four years he has been in the employment of Captain Towns, having brought the natives now on Townsville plantation.

Parties favouring Henry Ross Lewin with orders may rely on having the best and most serviceable natives to be had amongst the islands.

TERMS: £7 each man.

Henry Ross Lewin's claimed knowledge of the habits of the natives was not sufficient to avoid retribution at their hands; the man-stealer was subsequently put to death by islanders in the New Hebrides. Another disreputable blackbirder was a former medico — Dr. Carl Murray — who was later arrested for ordering the massacre of seventy kanakas on his schooner. Dr. Murray's father publicly disowned his infamous son. In a letter to the *Sydney Morning Herald* he said:

'As regards Dr. Murray, whom I have for years cut off as a disgrace to creed, country and family, your condemnation of that cruel unhappy being I fully endorse. May I add that although opposed to capital punishment on principle, if any of the *Carl* crew murderers ever ascend the gibbet for the seventy kidnapped and cruelly slaughtered poor Polynesians, Dr. Murray should be the first.'

But the former Melbourne medico escaped punishment. Nine of those on board his 256-ton brig *Carl* were eventually charged with murder, but only two were convicted. Even these were not executed, while Murray himself turned Queen's evidence and so defeated justice.

Most notorious of the blackbirders was William Henry Hayes, better known as 'Bully' Hayes. He also engaged in gun-running and piracy ranging the Pacific from San Francisco to the China Coast. His career was a much longer one than most of his contemporaries, hence his exploits have made him famous — or infamous — to this day. Hayes was a tall, powerfully-built man endowed with good looks, a full beard giving him a picturesque, swashbuckling appearance. He was always well-dressed and, unlike most of his fellows, was a strict teetotaller. An American Encyclopedia has this entry concerning Bully Hayes:

'Born William Henry Hayes. His father was a bargeman on the Mississippi, and young William Henry worked with him until he was about 18, when he ran away to sea taking with him 4,000 dollars belonging to Hayes senior. Married when he was 20, but deserted his wife after a few weeks and went to San Francisco with a second "wife". Here he was caught cheating at cards, and in the brawl that followed one of the gamblers cut off Hayes' ears. Leaving his "wife", Hayes embarked on a career of piracy, outwitting the British, American, French, Spanish, Dutch and German law. By audacious swindling and trickery he got command of various trading vessels which he later sold in various ports to unsuspecting buyers. He looted cargoes, and for many years was engaged in the slave traffic, becoming the most notorious "blackbirder" in the Pacific.'

No mention is made of his Australian activities, which were many and highly colourful. In 1857 Hayes landed in Adelaide where he met a rich and pretty widow, Amelia Littleton, who fell for his charms. He led her to the altar and, after obtaining considerable money from her, disappeared shortly afterwards. Knowing that the Australian police authorities were hot on his trail, the buccaneer made for New Zealand where he 'married' Rona Buckingham. Soon afterwards in company with Bully on a voyage to Nelson she disappeared overboard.

A favourite trick of his was to vanish for a few months and spread rumours about the islands that he was dead. Then he would come to light afar off and begin his piracy all over again. The *Sydney Morning Herald* of January 6, 1860, published an article entitled 'The Story of a Scoundrel' in which the writer described Hayes as 'one of the greatest rascals that ever went unhung'. Shortly afterwards Bully sent this sanctimonious letter to the editor protesting that he was not as bad as he had been painted:

Sir:

In the *Sydney Morning Herald* of January 6, 1860, you have published an article representing myself.

Much as I am pained by the perusal of the libel, I feel some satisfaction in the reflection that I have friends in many places who can, on oath if necessary, contradict the gravest charges. This fact, coupled with my own conscious innocence, supports me in my trying adversities.

It is easy to string together a pack of lies, or innocent truths worked up into odious fiction, to gratify the morbid tastes of a depraved public.

The article said I would not dare to show my face in Australia, the Far East and elsewhere. This prediction would be fulfilled if the numerous charges so ruthlessly levelled against me were true. I have nothing to dare. However, I freely confess that had even half those lying

tales been true I would not dare to face Australia again,
or indeed any of my former scenes.

Yours, etc.,

William Henry Hayes.

At least Bully's letter revealed that the gift of the gab
could be added to his many accomplishments. He met his
death in 1876 while navigating a stolen vessel (he also stole
the owner's wife and took her on a Pacific cruise) through
the Line Islands. In an argument with his cook, Hayes
kicked him severely and, according to the cook, rushed
below to get a revolver to finish him off. When he came
on deck again the cook was waiting for him at the com-
panion-way with the iron handle of the tiller. He struck
hard — so hard that the redoubtable Bully ceased to exist.
The cook couldn't believe that he was truly defunct. When
careful investigation assured him that such was really the
case, he tied the body to a small anchor and committed
it to the deep, remarking thankfully, but a little fearfully,
'For sure he's dead this time!'

In 1868 the Queensland Government passed an Act to
control the recruiting of kanakas for labour in Queensland
and to supervise the conditions of their employment.
Natives could not be brought to Australia except under
licence, and bonds were required of all persons wishing
to import labourers and of the masters of recruiting vessels.
The fallacy of the Act was shown when the captain of the
Daphne and his supercargo were charged with having
double the number of natives the vessel was licensed to
carry. No conviction was obtained and the court held that
according to law the natives were not slaves.

Missionary influence stirred up considerable agitation to
suppress the blackbirders and British pressure was brought
to bear on the Queensland Government. The British Navy
at one time had five men-o'-war patrolling the Pacific to
try to clean up the slave trade. A Royal Commission decided
that all native recruiting should cease in 1891, but the following year the order was rescinded on the grounds that

no substitute labour was available. The blackbirders were quickly back in the business.

In 1901, when the Commonwealth came into being, the Federal Parliament passed an Act authorizing the deportation of any kanakas found in Australia after 1906. After December of that year about 3,600 natives were returned to their island homes. Any who had married here or who had been in Australia for 20 years and wished to remain were allowed to stay. The final chapter of the ugly story had been written.

IO

Coral Sea Cays and Atolls

WOULD you be happy to live for twelve months on a tiny atoll with two other people (not of your own choosing) and not even an animal for company? There is never a shortage of volunteers for the three-man team which keeps Willis Island cyclone station always on the air.

Willis Island — a speck in the wide wastes of the Coral Sea, and only a few feet above it — is part of a group, the others being North Cay and Mid Islet, lying some 267 miles north-east of Townsville and about the same distance from Cairns. The islets were discovered in 1853 by Captain Pearson of the ship *Cashmere,* who named them after the owners of his vessel. About 500 yards long and half that distance in width, Willis Island is the site of an important wireless and meteorological station established in 1921. It has been of great value for weather forecasting, especially in North Queensland, since it warns the mainland of the approach and direction of cyclonic storms several hours in advance of Queensland coastal stations.

Harry Hicks, senior officer-in-charge on Willis Island for Overseas Telecommunications Commission, is enthusiastic about life on this Robinson Crusoe Island. So much so that he has spent six terms of twelve months on the island. Burned very brown ('that's because we never wear anything but shorts, and never a hat'), Mr Hicks had this to say on returning to Sydney:

'No day is really typical, because each can bring its own problems and difficulties. Routine chores — like cooking and cleaning-up — are of course arranged on a weekly basis.

'But perhaps I'd better explain first of all that the three of us cook week and week about. The food? Well, we bake our own bread. I have been baker for the last twelve months, because I have two brothers in the trade, and they put me wise to what yeast will — and will not — do.

'I baked a 4-lb. loaf and about a dozen rolls. That lasted us a week and there was always biscuit to fall back on if we ran short. We have every tinned food you can possibly imagine: the commission never stints on that sort of thing. In fact, our main storeroom looks exactly like any suburban grocer's shop — except that I'd bet our range of food is even greater.

'Of course, tinned food gets terribly monotonous, so we help the menu along with fish and turtle. There is wonderful fishing at Willis Island — but you have to be careful, because we are only 26 feet at our highest level above the sea. And I've seen as many as 100 sharks, from 10 to 14 feet, congregated off a spot where one of our team has been fishing, waiting for one false step.

'But you soon learn to watch out, and the fishing is excellent. We get parrot fish, trevally, Spanish mackerell, striped marlin and red bass as our staple fish diet. Turtles are our mainstay for fresh meat from November to March, when they come ashore every eight days to lay their eggs. Green turtles weigh about 300 lbs., and are simple to catch. You merely flip them on to their backs.

'At the end of four days, the meat is as tender as the best chicken. We have turtle roast, seasoned, curried and grilled. And, of course, we have crayfish by the bucket-load. They, too, are very easy to catch.

'We have our own supplies of tobacco and cigarettes, but no liquor. Willis Island is a dry station. It has to be. Imagine the effect of alcohol on a man whose nerves may fail him because of loneliness! To avoid any difficulty over particular brands of cigarettes or tobacco, the rule is for the officer to make his own choice before leaving the mainland, and his quota is brought to the island by the *Leeuwin,* our supply ship. Our met. officer, Bryan O'Connor, of Melbourne (he did a first-class job during Cyclone Clara), brought 10,000 cigarettes to Willis — and he was down to his last packet when he was relieved!

'Our greatest problem? Boredom! Certainly there's plenty to do on the technical side. Apart from routine met. work we receive and pass on messages to ships whose wireless gear may be temporarily out of order, and which can only transmit on a low frequency. We have a good library, an excellent radiogram with lots of records, and, of course, our short-wave receiver.

'We play cards, scrabble, chess, carpet-bowls, darts or table tennis. There is no lack of entertainment that way — the commission sees to it that our amenities are the best possible.

'Quarrels? Very seldom indeed. Naturally, a man can wake up with a grouch on Willis, the same as he does on the mainland (but not through the same self-inflicted wounds!). We know the symptoms, so we slip away for a bit of quiet fishing, or a stroll along the atoll.

'If you are a bird fancier, Willis will delight you. Terns, gannets, frigate birds, landrails, golden plover, cranes, ibis, cormorants, plus dozens of other species that stay with us when blown off their course on migration, until they've recovered.

'Arguments? Sometimes. That's why I insisted on an encyclopedia! Look it up, and there's the answer. But you still get the occasional chap who'll reply disgruntedly, "Yes — but that's only THEIR opinion!"

'Don't get the idea our Robinson Crusoe island is a sort of twelve-months long "lost-week-end". It isn't. We've no snakes, no rats, no mosquitoes, only a very, very few flies. But lots of cockroaches. We've no postman to worry us — although we're allowed to send — and receive — without cost, a hundred words a week, so we keep well in touch with our families. And . . . of course, we NEVER get any bills!'

The Coral Sea is the breeding ground of cyclones, and, despite the excellence of the work of the Willis Island station, many people in North Queensland are urging the

*Escaped convicts and 'blackbirders' used the waters of
Whitsunday passage*

Island aircraft over Pentecost Island, Great Barrier Reef

Weird fingers of coral are exposed by the low tide, Great Barrier Reef

installation of modern radar cyclone detecting equipment at as many points surrounding the Coral Sea as practicable. That portion of the Coral Sea between Willis Island, Cairns, Thursday Island, and Samarai is approximately 80,000 square miles in extent, and in this vast area there is not one observer unless there happens to be a ship crossing it, which is very occasionally these days.

The cost of establishing several such stations would be negligible with the cost of ruined homes occasioned by even a moderate 'blow'. It would be almost impossible to compute the cost of a cyclone such as the one which laid waste almost the entire town of Babinda. One mighty 'puff' of wind laid a complete train of railway carriages flat on its side without breaking the couplings. In the same year damage at Mackay reached an estimate of £1,000,000 with considerable loss of life. A fifty-foot tidal wave roared inland in the wake of the cyclone, completing the destruction.

I learned that most of the tropical cyclones which effect Queensland come from the East and approach the coast as a rule somewhere between Townsville and Princess Charlotte Bay. Many recurve before striking the coast and pass to the southward without doing damage. A few which originate well to the northward have been known to pass through Torres Strait or across the northern portion of Cape York Peninsula eventually to strike the Northern Territory coast on the western side of the Gulf of Carpentaria. Others have recurved inland in Queensland and caused great damage before again passing out to sea as far south as northern New South Wales. Most cyclones decline in intensity once they cross the coast, but usually cause extensive flooding inland.

There are many natural signs of an approaching cyclone. A sure warning is the ocean swell which radiates in all directions from the storm centre and is an invaluable guide to a shipmaster outside the protection of the Great Barrier Reef. However, except at very high tide, little swell may be felt within this great breakwater and what swell is felt as a rule is so broken up by its passage through the reef openings that it is difficult to gauge its true direction.

87

Long, thin cirrus stratus clouds which radiate from the top of the storm centre are a fairly good indication of the direction of the 'blow'. The presence of sea birds sitting closely huddled together in a long line close to the water's edge at a time of day when they would normally be wheeling about in search of food, is another cyclone warning. Also the presence of frigate birds· near the coast or in areas where they are not usually seen.

The Coral Sea islets, or cays, beyond the Great Barrier Reef are of three types: unvegetated islets formed of coral-sand and shingle, islets covered with low grass tussocks and other ground vegetation, and islets supporting both low herbage and trees. Practically all of them are unsuitable for human occupation; they are no more than a few hundred yards long and perhaps 10 feet high, and generally devoid of permanent fresh water. A few sea birds nest on the bare islets, while the others support large numbers of sooty terns, noddies, frigate birds, mutton-birds and other species.

Because of their unspoilt nature, however, they are of considerable scientific interest. When the naval survey ship H.M.A.S. *Gascoyne* visited the Coral Sea in 1961, stopping at no fewer than 44 cays, it carried six Australian scientists. This visit completed a survey — started in September, 1960 — of the natural history of the cays. So far as is known, some of the cays visited had never before been landed on by man. The expedition found a total of twelve species of sea birds breeding on the cays. Frigate birds of two species were studied in detail. These birds harry the three kinds of boobies which nest on the cays, and force them to disgorge flying fish and squid. Frigate birds are quite able to catch their own fish if necessary, but would rather let the boobies do it for them. The red-footed booby, previously considered rare, was found in large numbers.

'Booby' is an old name for a species of the gannets, believed to have been derived from the Portuguese *bobo*, a fool, and based upon the indiscreet trustfulness of the birds when nesting. It is said, too, that the birds were so-called because of their habit of blundering clumsily into the yards and masts of sailing ships.

A collection of birds, insects, marine life and plants obtained by the *Gascoyne's* scientists have now been deposited at the Australian Museum, the Queensland Museum, the West Australian Museum, and the C.S.I.R.O. in Canberra. 'The results of the trip,' says a report on the expedition's work, 'will serve as a basis for future research in the area and may be considered as a kind of stocktaking and indication of the opportunities for future detailed scientific research.'

One of the cays visited, Bird Islet, at the eastern end of Wreck Reef, witnessed three shipwrecks, and the sinister reef itself was the scene of two other sea disasters. Vessels wrecked on Bird Islet were the schooners *Harp* and *Anne* and the brigantine *Wolverine*. Wreck Reef was so named after the *Porpoise* and the *Cato* were lost there in 1803. Ninety-four survivors were cast up on what is little more than a sandbank, and were eventually rescued after Matthew Flinders, a passenger on the *Porpoise,* had sailed to Sydney in a cutter and obtained help.

For those who would like to make a day visit to a coral cay to observe bird life at close hand, I have no hesitation in recommending Michaelmas Cay, one of the little-visited areas of the Great Barrier Reef, and known as the 'Isle of Terns'. Picture a sand cay that is little more than a large sand bank, with a total size of about two hundred yards square. This cay rises no more than ten feet above sea level, and is covered for the most part by vegetation barely exceeding a foot in height including a herbage with small pink, yellow and blue flowers. At times this speck of land is a moving mass of nesting birds. Here then, is renowned Michaelmas Cay, the coral islet which gained world fame as the site of the first boring operations undertaken in an endeavour to ascertain the nature of the foundations of coral reef formations. The cay is located some 26 miles north of Cairns, on Michaelmas Reef. It forms a relatively accessible island for those who wish to see at close quarters the breeding habits of many thousands of birds — mostly terns — and is a sight which once seen is never likely to be forgotten, even by the least observant.

Michaelmas Cay, with its neighbouring islets, has for some years been declared a sanctuary for birds, so that these may be expected to find permanent refuge there. All of these islets, including the sand on their beaches and the surrounding coral reef, are entirely composed of the detritus of coral. Upola Bank is the best known of Michaelmas Cay's neighbours serving as a similar rookery for birds.

During the tourist season a chartered launch occasionally takes visitors to Michaelmas Cay. The passengers can scarcely believe their eyes as they near the white foreshores and see the multitude of birds on the isle and hovering above it. Going ashore they are still more astonished to find that the small birds, instead of retreating, close in on the visitors and even tumble over each other to get closer to the humans and satisfy their curiosity. Nor do they show any fear if picked up and fondled. One has to walk very carefully over the ground to avoid treading on the fluffy little creatures which are too young to fly.

Yet even at the too-young-to-fly stage they are seemingly never too young to swim and the fearless little balls of fluff bob up and down on the gentle rollers lapping the beach, or propel themselves on the water with rapid foot action. A remarkable sight, too, is to see the just-hatched chicks clustered in tight masses of many thousands, but all in groups of similar colourings — soft yellows and pale browns — yet never mixing. Above them fly the parent birds performing frantic aerobatics to the accompaniment of an ear-splitting din.

There are 16 species of terns, or sea-swallows, in Australia. Although classed as sea-gulls in popular parlance, they differ markedly from gulls in appearance and habits. Gulls are scavengers, with shortish, rounded bills and rounded wings and tail; terns have sharp, pointed beaks, pointed wings and forked tails, and live entirely on fish, for which they dive while flying.

As on Michaelmas Cay, terns usually breed in colonies on small islands or sandbanks, placing their eggs in a hollow on the ground. The most numerous species are the sooty terns and the white-capped noddies. The latter are unusual among terns in that they build a nest of seaweed or leaves on the tops of bushes or shrubs. The noddy terns have the curious habit of filling their nests with such hard and irregular objects as broken pieces of coral, shells, and so on. A conchologist told the writer that he was able, by examining the nests, to gather quite a collection of shells, most in good condition, and which he was unable to discover on the beach.

Some of each of the species of birds on Michaelmas Cay are always on the wing, day and night, and their cries are likewise incessant; not a minute during daylight or dark is there any cessation. When the birds take to the air their numbers form such clouds as to be visible several miles away, whilst their clamour is audible at a considerable distance out to sea.

Although the terns take to the water shortly after they are hatched, not until they are fully fledged are they escorted down to the beach to make their first efforts at flight. Then large numbers of the birds, in almost regimental order, gather on the beach at the edge of the waves around the greater part of Michaelmas Cay, in readiness for the flight.

The crested terns, unlike the sooty and noddy terns, are not permanent residents of Michaelmas but come to the isle for the breeding season only, arriving about November or December, and departing about February. A curiosity concerning the crested terns is the uniformity of the spacing between each individual nest, and the fact that when on the nest every bird faces in the same direction. Unless the birds are disturbed, every nest is occupied, and it is only at certain intervals that they all depart in flocks in search of food, to return together in similar fashion a short period later. The crested terns are apparently quiet, though alert, birds and do not evince the restless activity displayed by the other inhabitants who are continually flying all over the island. Even those who normally profess little interest in the charms of natural history could scarcely be unimpressed by the bird life on Michaelmas Cay.

11

The Reef Pilots

THE countless coral and other islands, the reefs, the cays, the atolls covering a unique area of 80,000 square miles off the eastern coast of Queensland are a tremendous hazard to marine navigation. Yet one of Australia's main shipping highways lies along the waters of this remarkable maritime maze. Day and night vessels of big tonnage are piloted through 1,365 miles of the Inner Route or Steamer Channel. This channel between the Great Barrier Reef and the mainland varies from 10 to 20 miles wide and from 15 to 20 fathoms deep. From Cairns north to Torres Strait there is, just outside the Outer Barrier, a similar Outer Channel about 8 miles wide and 20 fathoms deep.

There is no part of the world whose waters hold so many dangers and so close together as those surrounding the Great Barrier Reef, hence the men who pilot the ships along the vast and perilous waterway need to be specialists. Nor is there any other shipping route in all the Seven Seas so lengthy as this one to be worked by one man without relief. Maritime pilots in other countries are seldom employed in work outside of a bay or harbour.

Not all vessels sail the full distance of the Steamer Channel — for example the sugar boats of North Queensland — and reef pilots are flown from their headquarters on Thursday Island to various ports as required to guide the ships past the dangers. During World War II the Barrier Reef pilots were given top priority for transport; no one, no matter how high his rank or importance, was allowed precedence to a reef pilot regarding seat vacancies on a plane.

To qualify as a reef pilot one must possess firstly a master mariner's certificate and then spend some ten years of practical study before being entrusted with the responsibility of the guidance of any ship. Even so, the most experienced of these pilots will tell you that they are still learning more about the vagaries of the tide, the haze caused by occasional sand storms blown from the inland, mirages, patches of coral slime and other tricky features. The advent of radar has been of great assistance to the reef pilots, eliminating the necessity of anchoring ships on stormy nights in certain areas, or during cyclones when vision is obscured by torrential rains. Not, of course, that radar can disclose a tide-covered reef.

The Great Barrier Reef and its perilous waters have never been accurately charted. The immensity of the area together with the continual coral building on the part of billions of polyps makes the task impossible. The ever changing pattern would necessitate a fleet of survey ships on a perpetual assignment. The Outer Reef, via the Coral Sea, to Torres Strait and which was formerly used by the sailing ships is particularly poor in navigation guides. Because of grave risk to shipping, this and other imperfectly charted areas are avoided. No surveys of many sections have been made for more than a century. Soundings made by Matthew Flinders are still marked on parts of the chart. Naturally, there is no neglect in keeping up to date the charting of the traffic lanes now used by shipping.

The Inner or Steamer Channel which extends north to Cooktown has many islands but comparatively few reefs. The position is reversed from Cooktown to the top of Cape York, and this is where the pilot must be ever on the alert, even to forgoing sleep. He cannot risk a cat-nap with the perils of reefs and coral patches thickly strewn in this area. Notwithstanding the use of modern echo sounders, there is the constant danger from submerged reefs and coral and which rise abruptly from the deep warm waters. When after several days aboard the ship he is guiding, the vessel nears Goode Island the hazardous work of the reef pilot is finished. He leaves by launch for his headquarters on Thursday Island which is close by and where he can catch up on some sleep and enjoy a spell of relaxation before leaving for his next assignment.

Captain Cook was the first man to experience to the full the unknown perils of navigation within the maze of the inner reefs. No one appreciates the immensity of the original east coast pathfinder's achievements more than today's reef pilots with their present knowledge and modern equipment aids. Little wonder that Cook's journey along that part of Australia is regarded as one of the greatest feats in the history of maritime navigation.

In 1770, during his voyage northward from Botany Bay, his ship stuck fast on what was later named the Endeavour Reef. After jettisoning much of his gear he got his ship afloat again and eventually repaired it on the coast where Cooktown now stands. To his concern he found the reefs increasingly numerous as he proceeded north, and it was with intense relief that he espied an opening through the outer reefs, by which he reached the open ocean. In spite of his genius of seamanship, wind and tide bore him westward again, and eventually his ship was blown back within the protection of the Outer Barrier through another opening, which he aptly named Providential Channel. Always ready and eager to face the unknown, it is worth recalling Cook's own words: 'The world will hardly admit of an excuse for a man leaving a coast unexplored he has once discovered . . . If dangers be his excuse, he's charged with timorousness and want of perseverance . . . if, on the other hand, he boldly encounters all the dangers and obstacles and does not succeed he is then charged with temerity. The former of these aspersions cannot with justice be laid to my charge — and if I surmount all the dangers the latter will never be brought in question.'

Since Cook's time many vessels have been wrecked amongst the inner reefs. But of all known wrecks there can be none which happened under such extraordinary circumstances as that of the *Blue Bell*. According to Frank Reid, Barrier Reef historian, the steamship was sailing into the entrance to Keppel Bay, near Rockhampton, on the night of February 11, 1877. All at once those on board found her rising up from the water. At first they thought the vessel had run on top of a marine monster, but then noticed that she was wedged in the crevice of a rock that was slowly rising from the sea some 25 feet above highwater mark. The ship was abandoned next day. Now known as Blue Bell Rock, there are still rusty bits of iron, relics of the wreck, to be seen on it.

The Royal Australian Navy recently charted a new shipping lane to help develop the far north of Australia. The charting provides a safe passage for shipping between Torres Strait and Weipa, in the Gulf of Carpentaria. The survey will be of practical importance in developing Weipa as a port for its great bauxite deposits, besides making a significant contribution to the development of northern Australia. The charting was carried out by H.M.A.S. *Warrego* and H.M.A.S. *Bass*. Working day and night to complete the project, the survey entailed charting a 10-mile-wide shipping lane from Booby Island south to Weipa.

12

A Day on the Reef

THE Great Barrier Reef is by far the largest of its kind in the world. In contradiction of its name it is not a continuous unit of a single type, but is composed of diverse coral islands, atolls, and coral reefs, the latter of all shapes and sizes, some submerged, others awash, on which a dazzling ribbon of foam presents an amazing spectacle. Others are covered with sand, shingle, and green shrubbery forever inviting to the eye. The Reef extends from near the mouth of the Fly River in New Guinea down the coast of Queensland to Breaksea Spit, about 300 miles north of Brisbane, a total distance of some 1,250 miles. When one thinks of such a structure being built up until it reaches sea level for so very many miles, and considers the minute form responsible for this formation, one can readily appreciate that it is one of the most remarkable geographical features known.

The builders, tiny jelly-like polyps, live in colonies. All true corals are sea-anemones that have acquired the habit of secreting a limy outer wall and a series of internal radiating limy plates. Each polyp builds around itself a protective hard outer coat of carbonate of lime, which it absorbs from the sea-water. The polyp multiplies rapidly, chiefly by division, splitting apart about a third of its length, like the branches of a tree. Each split section forms its own protective coat of lime, each in turn dividing again, and so on.

The reefs are built in suitable situations on a foundation of solid rock or of sand or silt, and the coral communities

96

are restricted to seas in which the average temperature does not fall below about 65 degrees F. in the coldest month. Reef-corals need light for growth and are not active in building reefs below 25 fathoms. They grow best in clear water and are sensitive to salinity; an excess of fresh water is fatal to them. Heavy coastal rainfall coinciding with an exceptionally low tide will kill them off. An adequate food supply is of great importance; the prolific coral growth along the tropical east coast of Queensland is probably the result of the equatorial current which flows south and brings with it not only warmth but an abundant supply of plankton.

The polyp may live for a day or several weeks, but when it dies the lime skeleton remains. In this way large masses of coral are formed and are continually being augmented and strengthened by sand, shells, etc. The coral on the outer reef near the open sea grows more rapidly, because the untold millions of polyps are constantly feeding on the even smaller forms of life in the ocean. Above the dead coral the living branches continue growing upward and outward. The live coral being nearer the surface of the water and exposed to light, is a riot of colour. The gorgeous hues and delicate tints give the illusion of gaily coloured flower gardens. Hundreds of different species of coral may be found in the formation of one reef.

When seas are rough, fragments of coral are broken off and are thrown back landwards, the finer particles being strewn over the bottom of the ocean towards deeper water, thereby broadening the reef and forming a fringe along the shore-line, which itself is broadened by the outward growth of the corals. A barrier reef may be formed by the surf rolling over the reef and washing away the inner part, where living corals are few, and where the original reef has been separated from the land by a shallow lagoon.

Some of the inner reefs have upon them islands (cays) composed of fine (sand) or coarse (shingle) coral, algal and other detrital material heaped up by wave-action to a little above high-tide level. Many of these have become cemented and stabilized and are now covered with vegetation. A few of the islands, such as Raine and Holbourne, have cores of old upraised coral material now as much as 25 feet above low water mark, and bordered by living reef.

What is an atoll? It is a ring-shaped reef of coral rising up suddenly from deep ocean waters and enclosing a lagoon. The coral base may be surmounted by one ring-shaped island, but usually there are a number of islets forming the ring, and these conveniently leave passages between them so that ships may enter the lagoon. Darwin suggested that every atoll had started as a coral reef in the shallow water round an island which was sinking. There is nothing strange in the fact of part of the earth's surface sinking; that is how Sydney Harbour was formed, and also how Tasmania came to be separated from the mainland.

Darwin claimed that an atoll would result if the ocean bottom gradually subsided so that the original island finally sank out of sight altogether. The coral, according to him, would naturally keep on growing upwards and steadily increasing in thickness. There would be nothing to prevent the coral continuing to grow for thousands or millions of years and becoming very thick, if its growth kept time with the sinking of the sea bottom. In this way the 'top' of the reef would continue to be at sea level or just above it, even if the ocean floor had sunk a long way.

Professor W. J. Dakin, Emeritus Professor of Zoology, Sydney University, has pointed out that borings made on the Great Barrier Reef and the atoll of Bikini Island (before the atomic experiment there) favoured Darwin's old theory. Scientists, however, would like more positive proof, and the coral atolls still guard their secrets. Nevertheless it is generally agreed that Darwin was right in his belief that the ocean bottom has gradually subsided whilst the coral grew and accumulated.

Coral fishes are amongst the most brilliantly ornamental of all fish life. Vari-coloured in most extraordinary and beautiful patterns, they are found in great profusion among the coral reefs. Blue, gold, green, scarlet, orange or black, they glitter in their magnificent palaces of coral surroundings. The colours of almost every living organism in the reefs are often gaudy to the point of garishness, but despite this the amazingly bizarre patterns of the coral fish make them conspicuous even in such surroundings.

Molluscs range from the giant clam to the smallest of cowries with a glaze like the finest porcelain. The giant clam — the world's greatest shell-fish — is found only in the northern part of the reef; on the southern half its place is taken by vast numbers of a smaller clam, conspicuous by the brilliance of its sinuous mantle edges. Clams are only found where coral abounds. There are seven known species of which the three smaller kinds burrow in coral rock and the four larger species lie unattached on its surface.

Best known of all is the giant clam, *Tridacna gigao.* Two valves of the giant clam in the British Museum weigh 154 and 156 pounds respectively. Savile Kent in his 'Great Barrier Reef' says that one as long as 14 ft. was reported on one occasion by Captain G. P. Heath, a Queensland Portmaster, from the reefs off Cooktown. The aborigines have always been partial to clams and other molluscs as food as well as the shells' utility. Flinders, when in Torres Strait in 1802, noted the use made by the natives of the giant clam shells as reservoirs of water. The islanders placed them under the shade of pandanus trees, leading the water that flowed down the branches and trunk to the shells by tying long slips of bark to the trees and allowing the loose ends to lie in the shells.

The giant clams are mentioned by Captain Cook, who used them for food for his crew. Incidentally, two shells of this species from the Barrier Reef are in use as fonts in the Cathedral of St. Sulpice, Paris. Together they weigh 550 lbs. and measure between three and four feet across.

The frilled or furbelow clam, *Tridacna maxima,* when it opens its valves displays an extraordinary variety of colours. The shell itself is a pale yellow, while the mantle when seen between the gaping shells displays several gradations of shade, from palest turquoise to richest ultramarine and peacock blue, or green, with black spots and markings.

The Great Barrier Reef and its islands are a paradise for the cowry collector, for there the brilliant polish (rivalled only by that of olive shells of tropical seas) and beautiful colouring of the shells are seen to perfection. Predominant are the little money cowries; the poached-egg cowry, pure white outside with a brown interior and a black animal, and prized by natives as a charm for fertility; the dark mottled tiger cowry, and many others.

The vegetation on many of the island-reefs has been derived from the mainland, through the agency of birds, winds, waves and currents. Large numbers of the coastal plants have seeds which are buoyant and so are easily transported by currents. The casuarina tree's seed is furnished with a transparent wing that helps its distribution by wind. The pisonia, another tree common to many of the islands, bears fruit which remains sound after floating in salt water for several months. The fruits of some of the palms have a covering of glutinous material which adheres to the feathers and feet of birds and so are brought to the islands. Seeds of other plants may be devoured by birds and later deposited in their droppings.

A day spent fossicking on an island reef reveals a world of wonders. To view the fantastic coloured corals, shells, fish, and sea animal life at close range is a glorious experience. It is necessary, however, to wait for a low tide, and one must have the feet protected in sandshoes or gumboots. A stout stick is also required for turning rocks over while you are looking at the sea life.

The most common of the corals to be seen is the dainty branching staghorn. Prominent, too, is the brain coral which lives in colonies up to 12 feet in diameter. Another very solid coral is *Porites*, which builds massive colonies as much as 20 feet across. Very prevalent are the blue coral, the red organ-pipe, and the mushroom. The latter is one of the few solitary reef-builders.

Inevitably you will see clam shells in large numbers, their beautifully coloured mantles in breathtaking variety. Boldly-coloured star fish, sea hares, the lazy beche-de-mer and bailer shells all await your inspection. Sea urchins are found in practically all parts of the world, but nowhere else are they seen in such variety and in such numbers. Nor in their own natural habitat are they so readily accessible to all who care to view them as they are on a coral reef. Urchins are so called for their possession of prickly spines used mainly for the purposes of defence; they have practically nothing else in common with the little land creature known as the hedge-hog or urchin.

If you happen to touch the sea hare it will give out a purple-coloured dye that stains your hands and acts as a protection from other fish preying upon it. The beche-de-mer will do likewise, only it will ooze a white substance which looks just like great white tentacles. Sea hares, so called because of their almost hare-like shapes, are flabby molluscs with two pairs of head tentacles. Some species carry a small shell internally on the back covered by the fleshy mantle; in others the shell is absent. All sea hares — they are from about 2 to more than 12 inches long — are hermaphrodites. When the breeding season is at its peak during spring and summer they appear in large numbers in shallow water, and deposit, with each individual spawning, large string-like masses of yellow or cream eggs, which measure many yards in length when unravelled and contain thousands of developing young. Some 10 days after spawning the young hatch out into tiny larvae which after a short time develop into miniature editions of the adults. Even while less than an inch in length they squirt out tiny jets of the coloured fluid as a defence measure.

Starfishes, or sea-stars, are common along all Australian beaches and in rock pools, but the greatest variety of species occurs in tropical waters. The beautiful blue linckia (*Linckia laevigata*) is a continual attraction to tourists of the Barrier Reef and its islands. It does not hide away in crevices and is therefore often on view. Another large, spectacularly coloured and sculptured species is the rhinoceros sea-star (*Protoreaster nodusus*), found at the northern end of the Great Barrier Reef where it lives on dugong grass. It is a large five-rayed sea-star, brightly coloured in dark red and white, and the upper surfaces of the body and arms are decked with a series of solid black knobs and spikes shaped like the horns of a rhinoceros.

The pin-cushion sea-star is another large, conspicuous reef species, in appearance like a pentagonal cushion, with the upper surface delicately coloured in shades of green or grey with blue or yellowish markings. It may often be seen on sandy bottoms on reef flats along the northern parts of the Reef.

All starfishes, or sea-stars, show a wide diversity in form, sculpture, and colour, but their beautiful colours generally fade when the creatures are preserved or dried. A great number have the orthodox five-rayed pattern but some species have more arms than this. None is dangerous to handle. A peculiarity of the starfish is that it possesses the power of self-mutilation and of regenerating lost parts. If caught by an arm in attack it promptly discards it and later grows another in its stead. Often a fossicker on the reef will encounter specimens which are in this process of regeneration. One species actually uses this ability as a normal means of reproducing: when its fully adult eight-armed stage is reached it will divide into two and each part, now with only four arms, will gradually grow four new ones.

Crabs are plentiful on the island reefs. The swift or ghost crab occurs in great numbers. The greyish-white to greenish-cream colouration suits well the background of sand over which it moves with great rapidity during nightly scavenging forays. When it is running, its body is carried high, and its ability to dodge swiftly makes its capture difficult. And you will find other large crabs, enamelled blue and green, scuttling madly into crannies at your approach.

Holothurians, also popularly known as sea-cucumbers, are common along the Great Barrier Reef. A few are beautifully coloured, but the majority are drab and unattractive. Some 158 species have already been recorded in Australian waters and there are probably many more species to be discovered, but only the beche-de-mer or trepang are of economic importance. Hundreds of thousands of pounds of trade has been done in beche-de-mer since the industry was first established, but today's production has fallen to

Mangrove trees on Howick Island. Scene of the Mary Watson tragedy

*A tramway runs from the 1400 ft. jetty at Hayman Island
to the Royal Hayman Hotel*

Cliffs at Hayman Island

negligible proportions because of low market prices. Prized in the Orient as a food delicacy, mostly to make soups, nine or ten kinds of trepang are marketed. The better-known varieties include Tiger, Lolly, Stone, Prickly, and Black, the names being self-explanatory. After collection they are gutted, lightly boiled, and then opened out and smoked till thoroughly dry.

Australia's tropical fishes have been celebrated by many writers and they are justly enthusiastic about those found in the waters of the Great Barrier Reef. The first white visitor to these parts, James Cook, described the 'multitude of fishes' he saw swimming amongst the coral at Palmerston Island (which he discovered and named in 1770) in these words: 'Their colours were the most beautiful that could be imagined: blue, yellow, black, red, etc., far excelling anything that can be produced by art. The richness of this submarine grotto was greatly increased by their various forms, and the whole could not possibly be surveyed without a pleasing transport, accompanied, at the same time, with regret that a work so astonishingly elegant should be concealed in a place so seldom explored by the human eye.'

Under stones on the reef, lying in wait for prey, live the moray or reef eels, which sometimes snap at waders. The stone-fishes whose spines may inflict fatal wounds are also found in such places. Resembling a piece of eroded stone, variously tinted and marked, looking just like a fragment of rock covered with marine growth, the stone-fish has needle-like spines which spring into action when touched. Carved models of the stone-fish are used by aboriginal tribes to teach the native youth where not to tread when wading upon reefs in search of food. When the poison glands and spines are removed this dreaded fish is said to be good eating.

Swimming slowly among the coral and rocks, displaying long feather-like fins, are the butterfly-fishes. They show an amazing richness and variety of colours and patterns. Characteristic of this family is the long snout and bristle-like teeth that are ideally modified for picking particles of food from the interstices of the coral growth.

To end your adventurous day on the reef you will bring home a collection of coral and cowries and other samples of your fossicking, but, best of all, a greater knowledge of the marine world of nature.

13

Stories of the Great Barrier Reef

MANY are the stories of treasure trove, tragedy, romance and adventure surrounding the island waters of the Great Barrier Reef. In a gale-force wind and a following sea, the *Lancashire Lass* was flying home at breakneck speed. It was the year 1890. She was laden with pearl shell from the pearling grounds east of Cape York, and she was headed down the coast for a North Queensland port.

Suddenly, looming ahead, was a terrifying sight. Huge walls of breaking foam disclosed the presence of a 'killer' reef. The *Lancashire Lass* was racing towards it, and the sea was running too fast for the vessel to alter course. In vain the skipper looked for a gap, but there wasn't one. Only a wall of thundering surf crashing across the coral reef from one end of the horizon to the other. Nothing could be done but to take a chance in a thousand — to plunge the schooner into it and pray that the surf might carry her over.

Madly the little craft flew on towards the reef and inevitable destruction. Then a stupendous wave thundered behind her. It lifted her up — up and over, dropping her down in the still green calm of the lagoon on the other side. Sails were lowered, the anchor dropped, and the schooner rode in safety.

The crew all thanked their lucky stars. But how could they find a way out again? They explored all round the island reef but they found no gap. Their only chance of escape was to cast the pearl shell overboard, lightening the

105

ship, and try to float her over the reef at high tide. The shell was sewn in bags and lowered into 30 feet of water, the spot being marked with a buoy.

At next high tide the *Lancashire Lass* just scraped across the reef. In a few days she reached her Queensland port and the skipper told the story. At once the owners fitted out another, lighter vessel to go and retrieve the pearl shell, at the same time engaging an experienced diver for the purpose. This ship reached the reef and crossed in safety. The buoy was found, and the diver went below.

Minutes passed, then the diver surfaced, making frantic signs for his helmet to be unscrewed. He was so excited he could hardly tell his incredible story. He'd found the bags of pearl shell, right enough, but they were lying on top of a huge mound of silver coins. To prove it, he took from his pocket a fistful of Spanish dollars cemented together by coral insects. Without delay, the crew began to raise the loot. There were so many thousands of silver dollars the schooner had to make several trips before all of it was salvaged.

How did these coins get into the lagoon? Could a Spanish ship sailing to the Philippines have encountered the same experience as the *Lancashire Lass* — but without her luck? And when her wreckage disintegrated, had she left behind her imperishable treasure of silver dollars in that very spot where the *Lancashire Lass* abandoned hers? The facts behind this fantastic story are ones we shall never know.

There is said to be a fortune in gold to be picked up near Nares Rock in the vicinity of Flinders Passage in the Great Barrier Reef. The steamer *Gothenberg* was wrecked there on February 24th, 1875. Only 27 lives were saved, 102 being lost. On board the vessel, which was on its way from Darwin to Adelaide, were some eighty miners, all of whom had large sums in gold in their possession. There was also £30,000 of gold in the ship's safe. Most of the miners were drowned when the ship sank because they refused to part with their heavy money belts, and thus weighted down they went to the bottom like stones. Their skeletons lie scattered about the wreck today in a hundred fathoms of water, far beyond the reach of divers.

The Whitsunday Group regions of the Great Barrier Reef are rich in stories of ill-fated sailing ships and trading schooners. Legend has it that a Spanish galleon lies at the bottom of Cid Harbour.

Palm Island, close to Townsville, possesses a curiosity that is reputed to suggest that treasure may be buried there. Growing on the island is an avenue of strange trees not to be found elsewhere in Australia. The trees are large and shady, in two rows. The individual trees are so evenly spaced that they were obviously planted by man. Though there is no direct evidence to indicate that Spaniards planted them, they are believed to have been placed there in days before Captain Cook came to Australia.

The Great Barrier Reef has witnessed many adventurous early mariners attempting to navigate its razor-edged hazards. The strangest and most remarkable voyage was in 1791, and the venture was prompted, organized and was virtually led by a convict woman, Mary Bryant. This open boat journey from Sydney to Koepang, Timor, was one of immense courage, audacity and endurance by the young woman and her escapee companions, all of them illiterate and handicapped by ignorance of seamanship. Yet without loss of life the party of eleven, including Mary's three-years-old daughter and baby son, navigated their six-oared ketch 3,254 miles through strange and treacherous waters in ten weeks. They were the first white people to enter unknown anchorages within the Barrier Reef and many of the rivers and bays along the coasts of New South Wales and Queensland. They were also probably the first to discover coal in Australia, since they burnt it in their fires when they landed at the entrance to the Hunter River. Along the Barrier Reef and its many islands they found plenty of fish, oysters, turtles, and their eggs, and on one occasion they caught a dugong.

Mary was a Devonshire girl of good looks and great resolution when she first met the man she eventually married. He was William Bryant, a fisherman who like many another in Devon engaged in a little smuggling when opportunity offered. Caught red-handed, he was sentenced to seven years' transportation to Botany Bay. While Bryant was in Winchester Gaol awaiting to be shipped to the new penal colony, Mary planned a bold bid for his escape. She obtained permission to visit him and during the twenty minutes she was allowed in his cell she dressed him in a bonnet and cloak which she had stolen and he walked out of prison as a woman. Her sacrifice was scarcely worth while, for Bryant was captured shortly afterwards. Mary also was sentenced to transportation to Botany Bay.

Both arrived in the First Fleet, but on different vessels. One of the early proclamations of Governor Phillip was that convicts would be allowed the privilege of marriage; William Bryant and Mary Braund's marriage is registered as No. 5 in the newly established colony of New South Wales. Bryant being a skilled fisherman was employed catching fish for the struggling settlement. Stores carried by the supply ships in the First Fleet were soon depleted, and with the lack of experienced farm hands there was little hope of making the settlement a self-supporting one.

The penal colony at Sydney was only three years old and facing a grave food shortage when Mary Bryant, fearing starvation, set her mind to thoughts of escape. News of the epic feat of Captain Bligh piloting an open boat over 3,600 miles of ocean encouraged Mary to further efforts. She persuaded her husband to obtain a rough chart, a quadrant and compass from the master of a Dutch brig in Port Jackson. A quantity of rice and pork was also obtained, but it was impossible not to conceal the getaway preparations from others in the fishing camp where the Bryants lived. So it was that they enrolled as many as the little boat could accommodate.

On the night of March 28, 1791, the party sailed through Sydney Heads and steered north along the coast. Having no firearms they were in constant fear of the aborigines as they had to land frequently to get water, but miraculously they survived the tremendous hazards of every mile of the voyage. When at length they reached the top of Cape York they had another thousand miles of open sea to the west. Dismal about the prospect of success, it was Mary nursing her baby and with her three-years-old daughter beside her whose optimism and confidence urged them on to final victory.

But freedom was not to be theirs. Reaching their goal at Koepang they represented that they were survivors of an English brig that had been wrecked. Their story was at first believed and they were received kindly but suspicion was later aroused and the Dutch Governor had them returned to England. The ill treatment to which they were subjected on the voyage to England caused the deaths of Mary's husband and the two children. In England Mary and the rest of the survivors were convicted again and sent to Newgate Prison to complete their sentences.

Some day the tragic adventures of Mary Bryant and her dauntless companions will surely be the inspiration for a great novel or film. Certainly James Boswell, the famed biographer of Samuel Johnson, was deeply touched by Mary Bryant's pathetic story. His compassionate heart was moved to do what he could to soften her fate. He visited her in prison — she was then only 28 years old — giving her financial assistance and helping her by counsel and encouragement. In recording what little is known of the later career of this remarkable young woman, Professor Pottle says: 'I know of no one whom I should more proudly claim as my forbear than that heroic girl who escaped from Botany Bay and was befriended by James Boswell.'

For all we know, the sad story of Mary Bryant may have had a happy ending. Not so that of the heroine of the Lizard Island tragedy — another Mary, Mary Watson. This, too, was a sea drama, one of the world's greatest epics of a woman's courage and self-denial. Yet the martyrdom of Mary Watson is unknown to the majority of Australians.

During a stay at Cooktown I made the 47 miles journey north to Lizard Island which lies within the Great Barrier Reef about 10 miles from the mainland opposite Point

Lookout. A beautiful island of little more than five square miles of area, it has green, wooded slopes, lightly timbered, white sandy beaches and a good anchorage on the north-west corner. No wonder that Mary Watson when she first went to Lizard Island as a bride of twenty-one was delighted with her tropical paradise. Her home had already been built for her — a pure white cottage made of slabs of coral cut from the nearby reefs. Even the cementing was done with white coral lime. The garden surrounding it was also flourishing, and there was a crop of vegetables ripe for picking — the work of two Chinese servants, Ah Sam and Ah Leong, engaged by her husband.

Mary was born in Cornwall in 1859 and her family migrated to Queensland in the 1870s. While still in her 'teens she conducted a small private school at Maryborough, and for a while was governess to the children of the Bowet family in Cooktown. There she met and married Captain Robert Watson, a beche-de-mer fisherman who had a fishing depot on Lizard Island. It was a prosperous venture, the seasons bringing wide varieties of fish and a good supply of beche-de-mer, a sea slug much in demand for export to the Orient. The young bride loved her new life and we can see by her diaries that she made her own days busy ones. Added happiness came to Mary with the birth of a son — Ferrier — and for a time she had for company her sister who spent a long holiday with her and afterwards returned to her parents in Rockhampton. Life filled with all the interest and beauty of a tropical isle seemed idyllic to Mary Watson. Her diary recorded the simple day-to-day happenings such as this typical entry:

January 1, 1881. Made bread and cakes. Gingerbread a success. Wedding ring slipped off my finger. Found it later in the knife box when laying the table. Made a flannel shirt for Bob, also two tablecloths. We had an early dinner and spent a long evening outside humming a few songs and enjoying the moonlight.

Time slipped by uneventfully until one day Bob announced to his wife that he contemplated establishing a second fishing depot at Night Island about 150 miles north-

110

west. Mary, secure in her happiness and with the two trusted Chinese to care for her and the twelve-months-old baby, was quite content to remain behind. There was nothing to fear, and when Bob Watson and his partner, P. C. Fuller, sailed from Lizard Island on September 25, 1881, Mary farewelled her husband from a nearby headland and returned contentedly enough to her little white home.

Two days later she wrote in her diary:

Blowing south-east gale. Ah Sam saw steamer's smoke in distance, bound north.

The following day's entry again referred to the gale wind still blowing, but the entry on the next day recorded the first of the tragic events that were soon to close her life. Unseen apparently by the little household natives from the mainland had landed on the island. Seeing smoke from a campfire not far off, Ah Leong went to investigate. He never returned; Ah Sam found his blood-stained cap and hurriedly returned to his mistress with the grim news. Help from Cooktown was most unlikely, and with only four days gone of a mission expected to last two weeks, Mary could not hope for an early return of her husband. She realized the gravity of the situation when she wrote in her diary for September 30:

Blacks at beach. Fired rifle and revolver shots and they moved off.

The position worsened on October 1st when both Mary and Ah Sam were wounded by spears thrown by four natives. The Chinese was severely wounded but Mary's wounds were slight. Her plight was now pitiful with the care of her infant, one servant dead and the other helpless, and no boat in which to leave the island. She made a desperate decision — a bid for escape in a four feet square iron tank that was used for boiling beche-de-mer. The clumsy little craft had to be prepared without the natives realizing her purpose. She put a few tinned provisions and fresh water in it, a cushion for the baby and a parasol to keep the fierce tropical sun off its face. Somehow, with what little help the wounded Ah Sam could give, she levered the tank down to the water's edge. And so, using two short roughly made paddles to help propel the unwieldly vessel along, the perilous voyage began.

Mary had left her diary, up to date, in her home but she continued her records in a new book right to the sorrowful end. Entries of stark brevity that make the tragedy all the more poignant.

October 2. Left island in tank used for boiling beche-de-mer.

October 4. Tried to reach a sandbank, but got on reef.

October 5. Looking out for boats. Saw none.

The next day the tank was refloated, and once more they were moving with the current. The entry for that day reads:

October 6. Reached an island to look for water, but found none. Blacks there, so waited for tide to float tank.

The island reached was Howick No. 5, one of a group of ten islets, 31 miles from Lizard Island. Along the Great Barrier Reef the currents are strong, hence the surprising distance covered in the clumsy craft. From time to time they landed on small islands, without finding what they wanted so badly — water. On October 7 Mary recorded:

Reached another island. No water. Cooked rice and clams, and stayed night. Saw steamer pass north. Hoisted Ferrier's white and pink wrap. No answer.

One can imagine the young mother frantically signalling with the baby's wrap, and her agony of mind when she failed to attract attention as the steamer moved out of sight. But never in her diary does she utter one word of complaint, show any bitterness nor reveal a trace of self-pity. Her entries are recorded simply and briefly without any attempt to dramatize the helplessness of the three people. The little tank did not leave this island. The closing scenes of the heart-rending tragedy were lived and died here.

October 8. Shifted tank to a kind of little lake. Saw no boat. Very cold. Blowing very hard. No water.

October 9. Brought tank ashore as far as possible on morning tide. Blowing hard. No water. Gave Ferrier a dip in the sea, and took a dip myself. Ah Sam and self very pinched with thirst. Ferrier showing symptoms.

October 10. Ferrier very bad with inflammation. Very much alarmed. No fresh water and no more milk (condensed). Self very weak. Really thought I would have died last night.

A note of optimism sounds in the entry of the following day:

October 11. Still all alive. Ferrier very much better this morning. Self feeling very weak. I think it will rain today. Clouds very heavy. Wind not quite so hard.

The following day the last entry — undated — was written by the dying mother:

Morning fine weather. Ah Sam preparing to die. Have not seen him since 9 a.m. Ferrier more cheerful. Self feeling not at all well. Have not seen any boat of any description. No water. Nearly dead with thirst.

How long after the pencil fell from Mary's lifeless hand we know not and we can only hope that death came quickly as a merciful end to her tortures. A bitter irony of the heroic woman's martyrdom was that her rain forecast was probably right. When the bodies of Mary Watson and her infant were found the tank was half full of rain-water which had come too late.

The first indication of the tragedy was a significant passage in the *Cooktown Courier,* reading:

On Thursday, October 20, the lugger Neptune, *when passing Lizard Island, saw a number of canoes hauled up on the beach. The door of the Watsons' home was open, and about 40 natives were wandering at will about the place. After reporting the fact to the Cooktown police, a naval party was sent to investigate. Further intelligence is awaited with much anxiety.*

Within a few days the naval party returned, after thoroughly searching the island, bringing back with them the diary telling of the attack and flight. It was not until three months later that the *Cooktown Courier* was able to announce the tragic ending:

With the arrival yesterday of the schooner Kate Kearney, *Captain Bremner stepped ashore and hurried off to the*

Cooktown Police Station to report a melancholy discovery. Some days beforehand he had anchored off the Howick Islands.

Members of the crew going ashore found a small half-tank resting partly on its side. Lying in it was the body of Mrs. Watson, the body of her child still held in her arms.

The little tank also contained a small pile of baby garments and food. Close by was a revolver, fully loaded and cocked, and a tattered parasol still open, used to protect the child from the sun, was also seen. There was a pair of roughly-shaped paddles that had helped to carry them a distance of nearly 50 miles from their home on Lizard Island.

A further search resulted in the discovery near some mangrove trees of the body of the Watsons' Chinese servant, Ah Sam.

Captain Bremner brought with him the diary of the late Mrs. Watson which tells the tragic story right up to the day of her death . . .

The final scene in the grim drama, made glorious by the heroism and sacrifice of a young mother was the public funeral at Cooktown on January 29, 1882. Hundreds of Chinese marched behind the coffin containing the bodies of Mary Watson and her baby. It bore a single wreath bearing the Cornish motto: 'One for all.'

Standing in the main street of Cooktown today is an ornate memorial — a waterless fountain — to Mary Beatrice Watson. Inscribed on it are these lines:

> Five fearful days beneath the scorching glare
> Her babe she nursed.
> God knows the pangs that woman had to bear,
> Whose last sad entry showed a mother's care —
> 'Near dead with thirst.'

Mary's two diaries are treasured in the Oxley Memorial Library, in Brisbane. There, too, may be seen her photograph taken in Rockhampton shortly before she went to Lizard Island. Preserved also is the tiny half-tank in which the three people made their unbelievable voyage.

14

Guardian of the Channel

MANY tropical islands arise from the opalesque and serene waters of Hinchinbrook Channel, but none is more impressive than the one which bears the name of Hinchinbrook. Named by Captain Cook in June 1770 after the family seat of his patron, Cook could not see the channel and used the term Mount Hinchinbrook. Not until the area was examined in 1819 was the island recognized as such.

Hinchinbrook Island's proud and majestic bearing is in keeping with its task of protecting the port of Cardwell, which lies roughly between Townsville and Innisfail. Its area is about 22 miles long and from 10 to 15 miles wide, with several spectacular rocky peaks, the highest of which is Mount Bowen (3,650 feet). The slopes are flanked with tropical jungle and forests, which include pine and hardwoods, and there are many shaded streams and waterfalls with crystal-clear bathing pools formed by nature at their bases.

Hinchinbrook has been proclaimed a national reservation, adding to Queensland's wealth of national parks, and so is not marred by settlements or the tourist trade. A favourite rendezvous with members of Bushwalkers Clubs (some have discovered and examined aboriginal camping grounds and have collected specimens for museums), the island's wide variety of scenery from its mangrove-fringed shores to the rugged lofty peaks is a challenge to the nature-lover and the adventurous. During World War II an American bomber fell a victim to the mist-shrouded pinnacles of Hinchinbrook and it was several years before the wrecked

115

plane was located. In 1960 members of the Ingham Air Training Corps erected a cross on the site as a monument to those who perished. It stands out as a landmark and can be seen by passing vessels.

Varying light brings additional scenic splendour to Hinchinbrook and its surroundings, each time of the day having its own particular charm. Moonrise and the rising and setting of the sun in the Channel are a never to be forgotten delight revealing much of the magic of tropical waters. Owing to the abundance of marine growth on Hinchinbrook, the island is the haunt of dugongs and turtles. No better place could be chosen to study these fascinating creatures.

The dugong is one of the weirdest and least known mammals in Australian waters. Its popular name "sea-cow" relates to the animal's rather bovine temperament and its habit of browsing on aquatic plants in the shallows. In appearance dugongs are like a cross between a pig and an elephant. The face is like a pig's, the body like that of an elephant. Their hide is an inch thick, they are eight to ten feet long, and weigh up to twelve hundred and fifty pounds. The colour varies from brownish to bluish-grey, the underpart of the body being whitish or flesh-coloured.

Dugongs have no relationship with the whales but share certain ancestral characteristics with prehistoric elephants, since they have the mammary glands and teats under the forequarters, a short but mobile proboscis, and short ivory tusks which are quite evident in males. Although they cannot move a step on land they are air-breathing animals, powerful swimmers spending the whole of their lives in the sea. Their bodies are somewhat cylindrical in shape with a big half-moon tail and a pair of large fore-flippers but no hind limbs.

A harmless friendly creature, the dugong very nearly faced extinction in the last century when it was wrongly proclaimed that the limpid oil contained in the internal fat of the dugong was a cure-all for lung and rheumatic complaints. A well-grown dugong yielded up to five gallons of oil. There was a time when north Queensland waters

116

were teeming with the dugong, but they are fast dying out. Sharks are probably responsible, for they are the chief enemies of the dugong.

Believed to be the animal which gave rise to the mermaid myth, the dugong nurses and suckles its single baby like a human. When wounded it cries softly like a small child, blinking tears from its eyes. The tears are treasured by the aborigines as having mystic powers and native folk lore has it that no female member of a northern coastal tribe may look upon a dugong until it is cut up and prepared as food.

Dugongs never make their appearance along the islands until after sunset, when they come to the shallow waters to feed. Like cows, they are vegetarians and feed only on a variety of grass called sea-grass which grows in big patches in the shallows along the mainland coast and about the islands. They usually continue feeding until dawn when they depart for the open sea.

Sharks relish dugong as food, especially baby dugong. A shark will often snatch a baby dugong from its mother's breast. The female dugong gives birth to only one baby a year; she suckles her young clasping it to her breast with her flippers. It is strange to see the mother dugong feeding her baby, both with their heads above the water. Although a female dugong suckling a baby is very easy to catch by means of a harpoon, it is an unwritten law among fishermen that it must not be touched. (Dugong meat is delicious and does not taste at all like fish but rather like pork.) Of course this consideration is not shown by sharks which often snatch the baby dugong, leaving the mother swimming in circles, a pitiful sight, vainly seeking her baby.

On Hinchinbrook you can be introduced to the female turtle only, for, as on other northern islands, the male turtle never come ashore. The largest species in Australian waters is the luth, or leathery turtle, *Dermocheles coriacia,* which has been known to attain a length of 8 feet and a weight of half a ton. The green or edible turtle, *Chelonia mydas,* is a vegetable feeder and is the source of turtle soup. It attains a length of more than 4 feet. Visitors to the tourist resorts of the Great Barrier Reef and the adjacent coastline often practise the 'sport' of straddling a green turtle, grasping its forelegs, and riding it some distance.

Two other turtles found at Hinchinbrook are the hawksbill *(Eretmocheles imbricata)* and the loggerhead *(Caretta caretta)*, both of which are carnivorous and rarely exceed a length of 3 feet. The horny plates of the shells of the young are the 'tortoiseshell' of commerce.

An introduction to the turtle world alone makes a visit to Hinchinbrook Island worth while. As the twilight fades from the waters and islands of Hinchinbrook Channel numerous mottled-green turtlebacks are seen floating on the surface of the tide. Presently the movement of flippers and the wagging of a long snake-like head can be seen and a turtle waddles awkwardly out of the water heading straight up the hard sand for the softer ground above high-water mark. She is bulky and slow, and travels ponderously. She puffs and blows but nothing deters her from her fixed purpose. Block her way, stand in her path, she gives no more than a sigh of distress or annoyance and keeps on going.

Eventually the turtle reaches the soft sand and decides upon a suitable spot. She then begins to dig. Heedless of any curious human beings who might be watching her, she refuses to be deviated from her purpose even by a flashing torch. The turtle digs with her flippers. She works hard, now and again pausing for a rest, then with a deep sigh of resignation begins once more to send sand flying in all directions. When a hole has been made large enough to take her carapace, or shell, she begins the most delicate and extraordinary operation — that of digging with her back flippers a perfectly formed circular cavity, twelve inches deep, as a repository for her eggs. She then settles herself down and lays one egg after another, up to two hundred in number, each as big as a golf ball. So interesting to naturalists is this feat that representatives of the world's important scientific institutions travel from many countries to witness the egg laying. On one occasion a party of scientists saw a turtle lay two hundred and eighty-five eggs in fifteen minutes.

This duty having been completed and the last egg placed in position the turtle covers them over with sand, smoothes the surface with her flippers, pats it down, makes a few indentations in the sand to camouflage the nest and, without further delay, returns to the water. She leaves the eggs and the baby turtles that will hatch from them to look after themselves. She never sees them again.

After many days of hot sunshine, the sand nest begins to stir. One by one, queer little round brown bodies push through — and unerringly make for the water. Nature has endowed these minute creatures with a wonderful sense which leads them at once in the right direction. Unfortunately, heavy toll is taken by natural enemies. Tiny as the palm of a baby's hand, most of them are eaten by waiting birds even before they reach the water. Others are devoured by hungry fish as soon as they take their first plunge. The lucky chicks that survive their enemies remain in the sharp corals and rock pools, never venturing forth until they are well grown and have at least a chance of matching the enemy.

Hundreds of holiday-makers seeking a tropic island have found rest, relaxation, and the unusual at beautiful Orpheus Island, fifty miles north of Townsville. Close to the enchanting Hinchinbrook Channel, it is one of the nearest Barrier Reef islands to the mainland. Its opalescent waters and glittering beaches fringed on one side with jade green vegetation and on the other by coral reefs, makes Orpheus the synthesis of all dreams of a tropic paradise. The stage is set with coral gardens, clams, and vividly coloured fish. Many rare and lovely shells make a walk along the reefs and rocks an experience long remembered. Bird life, too, is prolific.

The island was named by Lieutenant Richards of the *Paluma* about 1887 after H.M.S. *Orpheus* which was wrecked off New Zealand in 1863 with the loss of its commander and 187 of the crew. Orpheus can be reached by plane from Townsville, then by the island car to Lucinda, or by rail to Ingham. The final stage is by the island launch *Moana*.

Genial hosts Colin and Mrs Taylor (the former was a solicitor) are ex-New Zealanders who offer their twenty-two guests gracious living. All the expected comforts are there, the food (served by candlelight at dinner) is superb and is matched only by the island's hospitality. Electricity is installed and there is never a water shortage for the island is blessed by a spring supplying ample, clear soft water for all needs.

Among the outdoor attractions are trips to Palm Island, the Outer Reef, and through the Hinchinbrook Channel itself. *Riki,* a 17 ft. motor boat, is available for cruising and fishing in the calm waters around Orpheus, and dinghies are supplied to the guests without charge. Accommodation is provided in cabins and bungalows and is as comfortable as could be desired. The Taylors' distinguished guests have included Miss Vivien Leigh and other members of the Old Vic. Company.

Twelve Australians have joined a group of English families who are settling on an island Utopia, thirty miles off the North Queensland coast. The community was founded by a young English couple, Jeffrey and Christine Forse. Their island is Middle Percy, 70 miles south-east of Mackay. Twenty-one years old Jeffrey Forse and his 19-year-old wife began their experiment with twelve Australians, and are planning to bring out small groups of people from England building up the population of the island along with its resources. Over the years they expect the island to support at least one hundred. Many people in England have applied to join the community.

The Forse couple, after exploring many islands along the Barrier Reef, selected Middle Percy as the island of their dreams. 'The name Percy may not be very romantic,' said Jeffrey Forse, 'but we don't intend to change it. In fact we've grown rather fond of the name. There is plenty of fresh water, good timber for building, and the soil will grow anything. There are snow-white beaches, a land-locked lagoon whose waters abound in tropical fish. But with all this,' he added, 'it's not going to be a Utopia, at least for a start. It's going to be plain hard work.'

Middle Percy Island lies in the Outer Great Barrier Reef and covers about seven and a half square miles. From the sea it undulates inland, rising to a plateau 700 feet high. From the air the island is shaped like a kangaroo skin. Until the community 'paradise' venture, the island's only inhabitants were the owners, the White family, two brothers and sisters who had lived there for 40 years, and who have now shifted to the mainland. Insufficient finance is holding up the project at the time of writing.

15

The Whitsunday Islands

THE Whitsunday Passage with its 106 islands is of exceptional beauty. Whitsunday Island, and the passage between it and the coast, was named by Captain Cook as he sailed cautiously through it one Whit Sunday when exploring Australia's east coast. Today's shipping still uses the passage with its invariably placid waters protected by the outer reef from the Pacific rollers. The channel is about 20 miles long and with a minimum width of 2 miles.

Whitsunday Islands is a collective label which includes the Cumberland Islands and the Smith Group — islands of delight of which perhaps only a dozen are occupied. They are of varying size and appearance; 70 of the 106 islands are very close to each other. Some are true mainland formations, peaks of a chain of mountains rising from a base that sank deep beneath the sea many thousands of years ago. They are rocky and steep, of basalt or granite, rising up to more than 1,400 feet from small beaches and narrow strips of level land. The slopes are clad with hoop pine, eucalypts, ghost gums and red gums, while on the sheltered faces are creepers, wild orchids, and stag ferns clinging to the tree trunks. The beaches are shaded by pandanus and coconut palms, the rocks at the water's edge are clothed with oysters, and banksias and mangroves line the inlets. There are other islands, flat and grassy, in this collective tropical group stretching more than 90 miles from Brampton Island in the south to Hayman Island in the north.

For 10 months of the year the Whitsunday islands — like

most of the Queensland coast — enjoy fine, sunny weather, with clear skies. At night the temperature drops 10 to 15 degrees. February and March are the cyclone months, when the island tourist resorts close down. The peak of the season coincides with winter in the southern States, but the end of the year from early October to December is the best time to visit the Whitsunday islands. Temperatures are higher then, but tempered always by the soft trade winds, the weather constantly fine and seas smoother than in the winter months. The spring months also bring the flowering trees and shrubs on the islands out in brilliant tropical blossom. The coral tree, casuarinas, bougainvilleas and hibiscus are at their best.

A fleet of three modern 112 ft. launches steam out of Mackay every Tuesday morning each with 20 passengers for a five-day cruise of the Whitsunday islands. The ships are fast, seaworthy and comfortable, with well-appointed two-berth cabins. The five days are spent cruising lazily around the many islands, stopping at the various tourist resorts in turn to swim at the beaches, and join the dances ashore in the evenings. Glass-bottomed boats are provided to view the coral grottos or row into fiord-like inlets. Plenty of time is allowed to try one's skill at fishing, walk over the coral grounds at low tide, and explore the Outer Reef. The diesel launches serve excellent food, have their own small bars, and carry two hostesses. Moreover there is plenty of deck space and fishing lines for all. Most fishing lines used in the Whitsunday waters have no more than two hooks on them. The fish bite so well that any first-time fisherman, or woman, can pull up two fish at a time. More hooks might require stronger lines and wrists.

Main tourist islands in the Whitsunday area are Hayman, Lindeman, Brampton, South Molle and Long Island. Hayman is the showplace of the Whitsundays, and the Royal Hayman Hotel is the gleaming answer to any who doubt Australia's competence to cater for tourists who demand luxury. I am not in that class and in fact dislike all fashionable resorts, especially when it comes to a tropical island holiday. But for those who are luxury-minded, Hayman

Island is strongly recommended. From the moment the gay, candy-coloured train meets each vessel at the end of the jetty, the visitor is treated right royally. The dining room is air-conditioned, carpets are deep, the wine is always served at the right temperature and the snowy napery is the best. A cold buffet lunch is often served at one side of the hotel's swimming pool, and guests can make a telephone call to any part of the world. For women guests there is a beauty and hairdressing salon, and the island shop sells clothes, shoes, beach-wear, cosmetics and tourist requirements. There are bowling greens, tennis courts, badminton, archery and a playground for children. Movies and a dance orchestra are provided, and there is always 'island' entertainment. This is dressed up along the lines of the Hollywood idea of Hawaiian and Tahitian atmosphere complete with names and customs. Why Australia's unique island world needs the make-believe of other countries is perplexing to overseas visitors and embarrassing to many Australians, including myself.

Hayman Island itself is about two miles long and three-quarters of a mile wide, with an area of 960 acres. Its well-wooded hills rise to nearly 950 feet and are a sanctuary for birds. The sandy coves and coral reefs are rich in fish, such as Spanish mackerel, coral cod and kingfish, and the island is included in Queensland's extensive national parks.

About 1928 the Nicolson family began taking paying guests on Lindeman Island. Simple grass and palm-thatched cabins were built to be followed by more cabins, dining rooms and amenities until today modern luxurious and gay self-contained cabins and lodges with hot and cold water, sewerage and telephones, line the island's beaches. Lindeman even has its own modern aerodrome, and you can fly direct to the island.

Brampton Island also has an air service. The introduction of the amphibious 'Golden Islander' flying boat ushered in a new mode of transport for the island and has reduced travelling time from 150 minutes to twenty minutes. Leaving Mackay the plane follows the coast off Flat Top and Round Top Islands and makes touchdown in a smother of spray exactly twenty minutes after leaving Mackay. The Busuttin family who manage this popular island resort were formerly sheep farmers on nearby St. Bees Island. Before the first tourists were seen in the Whitsunday Passage several of the islands were taken up as sheep and cattle stations. The well-known writer H. G. Lamond until 1933 had a station property on South Molle Island.

The people who lease the island resorts have become a community of their own, who talk by radio-telephone, call on each other by launch and meet once a month as the Barrier Reef Islands Association to tackle common problems together. Some of the families first reached the islands nearly 40 years ago, winning a peaceful, comfortable living with a few cows, and crops and fish but little money in the bank. They needed little. Through the years, friends, guests and the first venturesome scouts of the tourists found their way there for short periods. They returned to the mainland enchanted and spread the word.

Henry Mountney demonstrates the versatility demanded by the islands. When he took over the Happy Bay lease at the northern end of Long Island in 1949 he acquired an old, two-storey house and some grass huts. Since then he has built modern cabins — doing his own carpentering, installing hot and cold water systems, the electric wiring, the glazing, roofing and painting. He installed his own lighting plant, and when his growing guest-list pushed the water consumption high he cut himself a green twig and went water-divining. He found water, dug the wells, installed small petrol-driven pumps, and laid the pipes back to his main tanks. He has a skipper's certificate to operate his three launches which are worth at least £23,000. Henry Mountney is helped in his prodigious round of work by his three sons. With Mrs Mountney and a staff of 10 they can cater for 70 guests in single, double, or family cabins.

The drive to spread modern, gay cabins with built-in plumbing throughout the Whitsunday islands has not reached all the resorts — and for this praise be. Reg Brooks' Palm Bay resort on Long Island still wears the peace and quiet of the pre-loudspeaker era. The dining area is a log-framed, open-sided pavilion with creepers growing over big, green, glass fishing floats originally washed ashore by the tides and now hanging from the room's rustic beams. The only sounds from outside are of the waves breaking gently on the beach and the palms rustling in the breeze.

Whitsunday Island is the largest of the Cumberland group, but is not a tourist resort. It has an area of about 27,000 acres, and like Hayman and its near neighbour Hook Island is a national park. The highest point on the island is Whitsunday Peak, which rises to about 1,430 feet. Cid Harbour, on its western shore, is a picturesque and sheltered anchorage. Of the seventy or more islands in the Cumberland chain Whitsunday is reputed to be the only one on which the natives made a permanent camp. A tribe of about 100 aborigines had their headquarters at a flat in from Cid Harbour. At this ideal site there is a spring of limitless water and a perfectly sheltered bay close by. Sheltering caves are also in the vicinity. There seems everything needed for island life on Whitsunday — abundant game, wild fruits and vegetables, fish in plenty, and oysters all around the shores.

A group of four grassy islands lying in Whitsunday Passage in the vicinity of Proserpine are known as Molle Islands. South Molle, the main and most southerly of the group, and North Molle have been developed as tourist resorts. Mid Molle, the smallest of the group, is uninhabited. So also is West Molle, the loveliest of the quartet and my favourite reef island. About twenty years ago it was known as Daydream Island and catered along simple lines for a small number of visitors. Unfortunately, lack of sufficient quantities of fresh water prevented its development as a tourist resort and it closed down.

Daydream was the first coral island I had seen, and since my youthful days its enchantment has never left me. Returning from New Guinea by the *Bulolo,* in 1961, the ship passed quite close to Daydream and I came again under its island spell. Crested and black-naped terns were spreading their long pointed wings above the surrounding waters, their undersides reflecting the clear green of the sea. A cool trade wind was blowing and one felt that an effluence of soft whispering was coming from the thickly wooded shores. The island seemed even to faintly sing.

At the southern entrance to Whitsunday Passage is the Dent Island lighthouse, known to all coastal travellers and to thousands of tourists who enter this vacationists' playground. The island itself is about six miles long and narrow in width. Adjoining the lighthouse are a couple of solid-looking homes, the residences of the light-keepers. The tower was built in 1879, and its candle-power of 22,500 flashes every 2.5 seconds, 120 feet above water level. As the island is in a main shipping lane it is far from being isolated, and ship passengers always line the rails to wave to the keepers and their families. An international code signal is made to ships passing in daylight, bidding good morning or afternoon, as appropriate. The head keeper has sent greetings to many 'first-time' ships, on postcards bearing photographs of the lighthouse.

Of the lighthouses guarding the waters of the Reef, Raine Island's unique maritime beacon is the oldest. It is also the only one to be so constructed by convicts — twenty picked prisoners, mostly masons and quarrymen, were taken up from Sydney, the ship's carpenter being responsible for the design of the building. The first 40 feet of the 'Great Tower' is constructed with coral blocks bound with clam-shell lime, and above this is another 30 feet of super-structure of wood from some of the wrecked ships nearby. Alongside the beacon (it was unlighted and served only by day) a large tank was erected to provide a water supply for shipwrecked sailors. Coconut trees, maize and pumpkin were also planted for their needs.

Raine Island itself is a coral one, small and low lying on the outer reef about 60 miles north-east of Cape Grenville in North Queensland. The 'Great Tower', the fourth beacon to be erected in Australia, was built in 1844 to mark an entrance between the Great Detached Reef and a projection of the Great Barrier Reef. Previously a number of ships had been wrecked in the vicinity while attempting the passage. Raine Island entrance was used a great deal until about 1860, but thereafter, owing to its dangers, most ships avoided it. The island — it was named for Captain Thomas Raine, the shipmaster who suggested to Governor Macquarie the establishing of a packet service between Australia and England — is much frequented by sea-birds and has been declared a sanctuary for them. At one time ships used to call occasionally at the island to obtain guano, but the deposits have been worked out.

Important to shipping are the Low Isles, near Port Douglas, a group of sandy islets only a few feet above sea level. The coconut palm is the predominant vegetation, but other trees and shrubs have been introduced by families of light-keepers during the years since the lighthouse and its cottage were built on one of the isles in 1877.

When I made a visit there in 1963 I noticed the grave of the wife of one of the early light-keepers; she loved the island so much that she requested to be buried there. The head keeper and two assistants work in three shifts to attend the powerful light which is visible to ships twenty-five miles out to sea. Stores and mail are sent by launch every fortnight and, as there is no jetty on the isle, they are loaded into a dinghy to be brought ashore. Fishing is very good around the Low Isles and the tiny community is a happy one with no desire to transfer to the mainland. As with other lonely and isolated outposts in Queensland, the children receive their schooling by correspondence from Brisbane.

16

Popular Island Resorts

APART from the holiday resorts in Whitsunday Passage and the Hinchinbrook Channel there are other popular island resorts such as Heron, Green and Dunk Island. Green and Heron Islands are the only two places on the Great Barrier Reef itself where tourist accommodation is available; the others are so-called mainland islands, situated between the reef and the coast of Queensland.

Heron is a true coral cay and was the private domain of the late Chris Poulson in the thirties. His grown-up family now manage it as a resort island. Migratory mutton birds, herons, noddy terns, silver gulls and fairy terns share the island with the tourists who fish, aquaplane, relax under the palms and explore the coral reef grottos. An extraordinary sight may be witnessed there every year when a million mutton birds arrive on the island on the same day each October. Nobody knows how they set the date.

Dunk Island has been intimately described and made famous by Edmund Banfield in his books, *Confessions of a Beachcomber, My Tropic Isle, Tropic Days,* and the posthumously published work, *Last Leaves from Dunk Island.* These charming books drew world attention to the beauties of his tropical home. Dunk Island, small and delightful, lies fairly close to the mainland at about 75 miles south of Cairns and 100 miles north of Townsville. Its area is approximately 3 square miles of luxuriant vegetation, undulating in many parts and well watered. Lots of other islands are scattered about the vicinity, but, in the words of Banfield, 'Dunk is the fairest and best'. Cook named it after George Montagu Dunk, Earl of Halifax. The outside world first heard of its many species of birds when some of them were studied by the noted naturalist John MacGillivray and his observations published in his *Narrative of the Voyage of H.M.S. Rattlesnake* (1852).

The island was the home of Banfield from 1897 to 1923, and during those 25 years he and his wife lived in comparative solitude but great happiness. A former journalist in Melbourne, Sydney and Townsville (he was born in England), 17 years of overwork led to a nervous breakdown of health, and this was why he decided to seek a simple life on a tropical island. He built a home on Dunk, planted fruit trees and vegetables, obtained some poultry, goats and cattle; there were limitless fish in the surrounding seas. The pioneering work on his property entailed much hard work, and he had the physical disability of limited sight, having lost an eye through an accident during his youth. But the outdoor life agreed with him and he quickly regained his health. Moreover, with the initial difficulties overcome, he found leisure to study the flora and fauna of his island paradise. The varied natural life and the beautiful scenery provided him with inspiring material for his fascinating writings. Banfield was a sound observor who loved nature and had a hatred of the taking of wild life. Dunk was his 'Isle of Dreams — this unkempt, unrestrained garden where the centuries gaze upon perpetual summer'.

To the aborigines Dunk Island is 'Coonanglebar', and the older generation speak the name of Banfield ('The Beachcomber') with reverence. Since Banfield's time the aborigines have been taken away and placed on a reservation. 'The Beachcomber' loved the natives, especially the piccaninnies. He said that whenever a black pearl was found it was the soul of a little black child, and very precious. The last king of the tribe who inhabited this island is buried near Tam O' Shanter Point, seven miles across on the mainland (the point from which Edmund Kennedy began his tragic expedition of 1848). Old Nellie used to say that on nights when the moon is high enough to light the way, his spirit returns to the island and is happy again. 'The Beachcomber' and his wife sleep beneath a simple cairn on the island in the shadow of an ancient tree. This most storied of all the reef islands was bought in 1957 by Gordon Stynes of Melbourne who caters for thirty-nine guests.

Green Island, 15 miles north-east of Cairns and a favourite day trip from that centre, is luxuriant with tropical growth. Great trees, palms, vines, and lawyer cane grow in profusion, while its beaches all around are of fine white coral sand. The island, originally an outcrop of coral, has grown to its present area of 30 acres by the gradual deposit of sand and sea debris through the ages. Plant life washed down by flooded rivers on the mainland has been carried there by ocean currents, and taken root. Birds, too, have carried seeds and fertilized the ground until today the trees and palms and all the growth of a tropical jungle are found there.

Very lovely coral gardens can be seen around Green Island at low tide, and there is a unique underwater observatory — the world's only deep-sea one — where hours could be spent watching the glories of the world below the Coral Sea and its flamboyantly colourful inhabitants. Green Island also boasts the first theatre to be established on a coral island. Owned and operated by well known naturalist and author Noel Monkman, the theatre seats two hundred people and was built at a cost of £26,000. Films shown are those of the marine life of the reef, particularly the special features revealed by microscopic equipment, which is some of the best in the world. One could never hope to view the wonders of the Great Barrier Reef as are shown with these special colour films.

Captain Cook named Green Island after a naturalist with the expedition. Cook himself would surely be intrigued to hear the aboriginal legend of his landing in this region in search of water. The story is told in a series of remarkable aboriginal paintings on a great boulder at Koombal National Park. They depict his landing, the losing of an anchor, and other incidents and are of unique interest, well worth the trip to Koombal alone. Koombal is seven miles from

Cairns, and a rather crazy looking small boat takes passengers at various times to the reserve. There is no jetty and visitors are taken ashore in a row boat to Brown's Bay, gateway to the national park where Mount Yarrabah rises 2,000 feet of rugged jungle to overshadow this magnificent area. Koombal means 'native bees' and is an apt name with the swarms of wild bees to be seen there.

One's first impression of the bay, which is surrounded by rocky points, is that of many palms. In the foreground of the park itself is Palm Grove, with a pretty creek trickling through. In this undeveloped area, which has wonderful country for the bush walker and the fisherman, or the rugged type, there is a guest house and huts but there is no electricity and no movies, hotel, or such amenities. But for the nature-lover there are some delightful jungle tracks where you can see huge vines, tropical flora, and billabongs.

Worthy of note is Lady Musgrave Island, the southernmost island of the Great Barrier Reef. This a perfect coral atoll, having a coral enclosed lagoon with a single deepwater channel entrance. Being near the continental shelf the deep blue water goes to a depth of 100 fathoms. Game fish of many kinds are here for the catching. The water in the lagoon is as placid as a lake, and seabirds come there in thousands for the nesting season. Turtles frequent the sandy beaches to lay their eggs, and right around the atoll are many square miles of coral reef.

No one has counted the number of islands that lie in the vicinity of the Great Barrier Reef. They range from tiny coral cays scarcely showing above the water to hilly masses miles in length and breadth. Each island seems to have its own mood, its own individual charm and attractions; no two are alike. But no matter what part of the Reef you may visit you will find islands of incredible beauty. They have an absolute detachment from the modern world, so much so that when holidaying there one finds it difficult to recall readily whether the day is Monday or Friday.

Less than five miles from the shores of Townsville lies

Magnetic Island and its fast developing community of nearly a thousand permanent residents. For years it has been a holiday resort for many people in Townsville and western Queensland, and tourists from the South often included it in their North Queensland itineraries. A large number of Townsville residents built week-enders and holiday homes on the island and planned to spend their retirements there. Despite its close proximity to the city the drawback was always suitable transport to and fro; the waters separating Magnetic from the mainland can get much too rough to sail daily with safety in one's own small boat. During World War II, when the Americans had a base on Magnetic, there were negotiations for the building of a connecting causeway between the island and Cape Pallarenda on the mainland, but nothing came of the proposal.

Late in 1959 a daily commuter launch service was inaugurated and this was the beginning of the rapid growth of the island community. Modern shopping centres, two excellent hotels, educational facilities, taxis and a bus service are some of the amenities provided for residents and tourists alike.

The launch trip from Townsville takes less than 30 minutes in good weather. Leaving the wharf at Ross Creek the launches are restricted in their speed until the long rock-made breakwater is cleared. Around the approaches to this part of the waterfront are some of the warehouses and storage buildings, old and new, of the city's mercantile life, as solid as the trade they house.

As the boat clears the breakwater and feels the bite of open sea it surges into Cleveland Bay with gathering speed. Looking astern one cannot but be impressed by the tremendous industrial activity of Townsville's harbour with its massive bulk sugar terminal, oil tanks and shipping traffic. But the great island looming ahead is what claims one's main attention. A long curving white beach comes into view as the launch nears the first stopping place at Picnic Bay. Close as it appears, the skipper makes a wide detour as though going to by-pass it, but he is manoeuvring the craft around and between unseen coral reefs until he

133

enters the calm of the island's lee. Passengers and freight for this call are discharged at the jetty where at the end of its long length taxis and a bus await fares.

Picnic Bay seems to be the commercial hub of the island with its compact shopping centre, post-office, movie theatre, modern hotel and golf course. The launch continues around the island to its other port of call, Arcadia wharf, but many day 'trippers' disembark at Picnic Bay and travel by road across to Arcadia where they pick up the launch for the return trip later in the day. This is a splendid way of seeing something of the interior of the island as well as the many beautiful bays and inlets along its foreshores.

It is nearly 200 years since Captain James Cook, sailing up the Queensland coast on his voyage of discovery, concluded that the variations in his compass readings were being caused by the granite outcrops on the island. So he named the island Magnetic, and although since then the theory has been proved wrong Cook's name has been retained.

The triangularly shaped mountainous island covers 25 square miles and is a hiker's paradise with many bush trails including one that leads to the summit of Mount Cook, 1,628 feet high. Great piles of granite rocks and boulders give parts of the island a rather forbidding yet strangely fascinating remoteness. Many fertile areas produce a profusion of tropical fruits and these comprise mainly pineapples, mangoes and pawpaws grown for the Townsville market. Most of the permanent residents of Magnetic Island work on the tropical fruit orchards; the workers in the groves of pineapple plants wearing 'Melahini' hats woven from the fronds of pineapple leaves provide a touch of Hawaiian atmosphere to the scene.

On the road journey around the island one passes through virgin bushland and a magnificent blending of craggy hills, wooded slopes and a succession of quiet beaches with their pure white sand and cool opalescent waters. Rocky Bay is aptly named with its granite foreshores and rugged landscape that includes the tall and hardy hoop pine. Largest of the bays is Horseshoe Bay, a glorious two-mile stretch of gently curving beach and mighty headlands, with its

134

The air-strip on Dunk Island

Imund Banfield 'The Beachcomber' and his wife are buried on Dunk Island

Nauru Island from the air

Anibare Bay, Nauru Island

peaceful idyllic cove known as White Lady. Here little boats rock gently on the tranquil turquoise waters whose many islets stretching to the far horizon convey the impression of an inland sea.

Nelly Bay is the headquarters of three denominational youth centres and boasts a bank, post-office, store, bus and taxi business. It may yet rival Picnic Bay as the island's commercial centre. A natural amphitheatre of hills encircles the beach at Alma Bay, protecting it from off-shore winds. Titanic granite boulders together with vegetation of yellow and brown shadings and sometimes tones of heather, spindly coconut palms and pine trees surround the deep waters of the bay. The brooding hills abound in wild goats, wallabies and koalas, and these like the island's prolific bird life are protected by law from everything but a camera. Koalas are sometimes seen taking a nap on a bush track and roadside trees. Oddly enough, unlike other members of their family on the mainland, the koalas on Magnetic often discard their normal eucalyptus diet and feed on the island's delicious mangoes.

Arcadia is the average holidaymaker's dream. Everything is there for the vacationist even to a bowling green. Many holiday homes and guest houses can be seen among the palm trees, and at times the beach and surrounds are crowded with bathers soaking up the winter sunshine. Although I have paid three visits to Magnetic Island I must confess that popular beach resorts and anything labelled as a tourist paradise have no appeal for me. But whereas Magnetic draws week-end and holiday crowds to its main centres, a few minutes' walk takes one to an isolated gem of a beach, or an inviting cove, with little chance of seeing another soul.

Fish are plentiful in the warm waters of the island and rod and reel fishermen do well — the most plentiful catches being cod, coral trout, king salmon, emperor bream, sunfish, tuna and barramundi. For panoramic views of the island's topography, a climb up a former military supply road to the 'Fort' is richly rewarding. This is located near Magnetic's north-east tip and here were established two

American command posts. From the gun emplacement and the command posts (remarkable examples of the art of military camouflage) one sees a series of bays scooped out of the three sides of the island, each separated by granite ramparts of saffron, white and yellow, and clothed by forests of pine.

There is a sense of space, vast and liberating, as one looks out over distant Cape Cleveland jutting out to the sea, translucent and serene. Magnetic Island may one day well become just another outer suburb of the city of Townsville but nothing can change the magic of a landscape that is entirely its own.

17

An Island of Birds and Flowers

THERE can be few islands more attractive to ornithologists and lovers of wildflowers than Fraser Island on the southeast coast of Queensland. The island is a stronghold for birds and has been the subject of numerous articles by ornithologists; there is an abundance, too, of wildflowers, notably the white *Crinum* lilies and the beautiful rose-purple *Tecoma*. But the island's charm does not rest solely on its bountiful bird life and floral displays. Fraser is an untouched wonderland of great contrast with surely the most beautiful beach frontage throughout the whole of Queensland.

Glistening white, wide beaches, unsurpassed in a land famous for its beaches, their beauty unspoilt by tourism; swiftly flowing trout creeks and sparkling streams; elevated panoramic views which rival Sublime Point at Bulli Pass, N.S.W. — these are some of Fraser's joys. Then there are the forests of pine trees flourishing in the sandy soil of the southern regions of the island. Here is a forestry reserve with foresters' camps containing an area of commercial forest in the region of 65,000 acres. A comprehensive system of regeneration has been evolved, particularly in regard to eucalypts, hoop and kauri pines. There was a time when large sawmills were in operation, when Fraser Island had its township, school, a regular boat service to the mainland, and even an island train. But that was many years ago, and few recall those days. Today, the only inhabitants on Fraser are the Forestry Department's employees, the light-

137

house keepers, a few fishermen and the occasional nature-lovers who holiday there.

Fraser Island — sometimes called Great Sandy Island — guards the entrance to Hervey Bay and the port of Mary-borough. With a length of 77 miles and from 3 to 14 miles in width, it covers about 393,500 acres. The narrow and treacherous Great Sandy Strait separates Fraser from the mainland. The island is reached by launch from any one of the three sleepy waterfront villages of Scarness, Pialba or Urangan — a journey of about 90 minutes.

Queensland's largest coastal island, Fraser is fortunate in its water supply. The land is composed of a layer of sand-stone covered by thick layers of sand, and this makes the whole island a natural reservoir. Deep in the forest country is found the remarkable water vine which entwines itself around the tall trees and is as thick as a man's arm. When tapped it produces crystal clear drinking water, cool and refreshing. There are many deep freshwater lakes; the largest, Lake Boemingen, covers 470 acres.

Moon Point and Platypus Bay are picturesque areas, and in the south the shoreline is broken by creeks and sand-spits which provide landing places for local craft and timber barges. The seldom visited island has some extraordinary sand formations, one of which is known locally as 'The Cathedral'. Clearly defined is a church scene complete with white-robed minister, an altar, organ, and statues. Another is a canyon of magnificent Namatjira colourings.

The waters of Fraser Island and its surrounding reefs have been the scene of many shipping disasters, the most recent being a fishing trawler wrecked there in June 1960. The passenger vessel *Maheno*, once the fastest ship on the Tasman run, went aground at Fraser in 1935. At the time she was on her way to her new owners in Japan. The wreck lies half covered with sand on the edge of a lonely beach and is a favourite spot for fishermen, the fish sheltering in the submerged decks and companion-ways.

The island is steeped in history, most of which was made by ships. Captain Cook skirted its eastern shore in 1770, not realizing that it was an island. Cook supposed it to be a long promontory and named the northernmost point Sandy Cape, while the dangerous spit which extends for 20 miles to the north of the cape he called Breaksea Spit. Observing numbers of 'Indians' and campfires on the foreshores, Cook gave the name Indian Head to the only other promontory on the seaward coast.

Matthew Flinders in the *Investigator* landed on Fraser in 1802 and made a more detailed examination of the coast, but even he was uncertain as to whether it was an island or a promontory. He published an account of his visit there twelve years later mentioning among other observations that he found the aborigines to be sleek and well-developed, but made no mention that Fraser was detached from the mainland. It is thought, however, that Flinders obtained subsequent information enabling him to rectify the error.

In 1860 the island was declared a native reserve, and in that year it was estimated that the aboriginal population on Fraser was several thousand. Nevertheless, when it was decided to establish a mission station there thirty years later only about 300 could be mustered, and these were transferred to the mainland. The first whites to live on the island were probably escaped convicts who may have lived with some of the tribes. The first authentic account of whites landing there is that of the survivors from the wreck of the *Stirling Castle* — and this was a sorry tale, a story of a woman's amazing fortitude, a story of the miserable death of a gallant band of British seamen.

On May 15, 1836, the brig *Stirling Castle* sailed from Sydney on a voyage to Singapore via North Queensland. In addition to his crew, Captain James Fraser had his wife, Eliza, a native of Stromness in the Orkneys, on board together with his thirteen-year-old nephew. One week out from Sydney the ship struck a reef, believed to be one of the Swain Group. All aboard were able to take to the brig's only two boats — a longboat which took eleven people, and a pinnace which held the remaining seven. The pinnace was delayed in making a getaway when it was found that the captain's nephew was missing. A search of the derelict revealed the boy on his knees in his cabin, praying.

The longboat whose occupants included the Frasers proved to be unseaworthy, and continual bailing was necessary. Four days later Mrs Fraser (she was 37 years old at the time) gave birth to a baby which died shortly afterwards and was cast into the sea. Eventually the castaways in both boats landed on one of the Bunker Islands, and here the boatswain and six other seamen commandeered the pinnace and left for the mainland.

After taking a badly needed, but brief, rest and trying to do what little they could to make the leaking boat seaworthy, the eleven people decided to leave the security of their shelter to try also to reach the mainland, which Captain Fraser estimated was about fifty miles distant. For another two weeks they tossed hopelessly about in the patched-up longboat, bailing endlessly and expecting any moment that the crazy craft would founder. They came ashore at Great Sandy Island — later to be renamed Fraser Island.

As to the seven men in the pinnace: these had landed on the mainland near Wide Bay, and here they were made prisoners of a tribe of natives who, after stripping them of their clothes and paltry possessions, made them work for them cutting wood and doing various odd jobs. Two of the captives, a British sailor and an American negro, made their escape one night and set off to walk to the Moreton Bay penal settlement. In this they were successful, and when they eventually reached their destination they told Lieutenant Otter, an officer of the detachment stationed at the settlement, their story.

Meanwhile the Fraser party had also attempted to walk to Moreton Bay, believing they were on the mainland. They, too, were captured by natives and were subjected to inhuman treatment, torture and sometimes death. Mrs Fraser saw her husband speared to death because, through illness, he was unable to work. She witnessed, too, the chief officer of the *Stirling Castle* being roasted alive over a slow fire.

Mrs Fraser's own treatment at the hands of her captors was no less fearful than that of the men. Some of her sufferings may be understood when reading Lieutenant Otter's report, after a rescue of the survivors had been effected. 'The woman,' he wrote, 'was a skeleton; the skin literally hung to her bones. Her legs were a mass of sores where the savages had tortured her with firebrands . . . When we met her she had been for two days without food and had subsisted the most part of the time on a kind of fern root found in swamps. Now and then she would get the tail or fin of a fish when the savages had a superabundance, and then she was obliged to earn it by dragging heavy logs of wood and fetching water. She was not allowed in their shelters, but, naked as she was, she was obliged to lie out the whole night, even in the heaviest rains. This is but a slight sketch of what she went through. When we had got about halfway to our boats we were obliged to carry her. We did not arrive until next morning, when she begged for hot water, as she was anxious to restore her face and person to a natural colour. The natives had rubbed her body every day with charcoal to darken her skin.'

When Lieutenant Otter organized the search party, on hearing the story of the captive castaways, a convict named John Graham offered his services and was accepted. Graham was an Irishman who had been transported to Botany Bay for seven years in 1824 for stealing 6 lb. of hemp. Later he was transferred to Moreton Bay, and while there took to the bush. In his wanderings he stumbled into an aboriginal camp where, in his case, he was treated kindly and he lived with the natives for nearly six years. Tiring of being so long absent from white company he decided to give himself up, and so he returned to the penal settlement. It was because of Graham's bushmanship, and knowledge of the natives and their language that influenced Lieutenant Otter in accepting Graham's services.

The rescue party eventually reached the white prisoners and Graham had little difficulty in bringing in the men survivors — the second mate, John Baxter, and two ships' boys, Robert Carey and Robert Hanham. Mrs Fraser's

141

rescue entailed much danger as the natives seemed determined to keep her. Lieutenant Otter said in his report: 'Graham shunned neither danger nor fatigue, and on the last occasion he was exposed to very imminent risk by venturing into the large camp where Mrs Fraser was detained.' The natives looked upon the white woman as a curiosity, hence their reason for wanting to keep her.

Afterwards, the Commandant of the Moreton Bay penal settlement, Captain Foster Fyans, wrote: 'To Graham alone are we indebted for the recovery of Mrs Fraser.' Fyans sent Graham to Sydney where he was given a ticket-of-leave and £10 with which to start life afresh. There was a happy sequel to Mrs Fraser's great sorrows. She subsequently married Captain Greene, the commander of the vessel in which she sailed back to Britain from Sydney.

The first thorough exploration of Fraser Island was made by an expedition led by Andrew Petrie in 1842. Five years later Lieutenant Dayman of H.M.S. *Rattlesnake* sailed through the narrows in the tiny *Asp*. From 1860 onwards settlers began to visit the island to get timber; in 1863 one of these men, John Piggott, was murdered by aborigines on Seventy-Five Mile Beach.

Because of the number of wrecks in the vicinity of Fraser Island a lighthouse was erected near Sandy Cape in 1881. During the immigration programmes of the 1880s and 1890s a quarantine station was established in the lighthouse reserve, but this was subsequently abandoned. The island saw much activity during World War II when a commando training camp was built in the south-west area and an airstrip was laid out near Sandy Cape. Today Fraser Island is once more a peaceful haven where naturalists and nature-lovers find it a sub-tropical paradise urging them to return again and again to explore more of its grandeur.

18

The Pleasant Island

NAURU, a tiny island in the central Pacific just 26 miles south of the equator, has been in the news of late because there is a proposal to move the population elsewhere, once its extensive phosphate supply is exhausted. Oval in shape, about 12 miles in circumference, the island's phosphate-bearing area is estimated at 4,116 acres. More than 25 million tons of phosphate have been shipped overseas.

Nauru's location is an isolated one, its nearest neighbour being Ocean Island, 185 miles away, and on which similar phosphate deposits are found. In spite of its proximity to the equator, Nauru has a sub-tropical climate tempered by cooling sea breezes. It is not surprising that when it was discovered by Captain Fearn in 1798 he named it Pleasant Island, a name which was retained for nearly a century before it was changed to its present native one.

The island is administered by Australia under a trusteeship agreement with the United Nations — a trust held jointly by Britain, Australia and New Zealand. Since its first contact with Europeans Nauru has suffered greatly from the wars of civilization. The island was annexed by Germany in 1888 and proclaimed German territory. With the outbreak of World War I, Australian forces occupied Nauru in 1914 and remained in control until 1921 when a civil administration was substituted under a mandate granted by the League of Nations to the British Crown on behalf of the British Empire.

During World War II, Nauru was heavily shelled, first by a German raider in 1940, and the following year by

143

the Japanese. Five phosphate ships were sunk and considerable damage was caused on the island. Nauru was occupied by the Japanese in 1942, and during their occupation they shot the Administrator, Lieutenant-Colonel F. R. Chambers, and killed also four other Europeans who had remained on the island to care for the inhabitants. Practically all the able-bodied Nauruans were forced into slavegangs and remained so until the Japanese garrison surrendered to Australian forces in 1945.

The deliverers found the island and its people in a sorry plight. Most of the industrial plant and buildings and all the houses had been destroyed, every civilizing influence had been abolished, and the people were in a state of wretchedness and semi-starvation. The civil administration began immediately to restore the pre-war status; the Nauruans transplanted by the Japanese to other islands to serve as slaves were brought home and a rebuilding and rehabilitating programme was begun.

Coconut and pandanus palms are widely cultivated on Nauru but the land is not suited for agriculture. Much of it is coral formation, and the island itself is surrounded by a coral reef which is exposed at low tide. The removal of the phosphate leaves a rugged terrain consisting of coral pinnacles which protrude 30 to 50 feet above the floor of the old coral formation.

There is no harbour at Nauru and the phosphate ships have to be moored outside the reef to deep-sea buoys. The problem of loading was solved by the construction of huge cantilever trestles which swing across the reef and empty the phosphate direct into the ships' holds. A light railway conveys the phosphate from the interior to the loading point. Before World War II labour was supplied by indentured Chinese, but in the post-war years Gilbert and Ellice islanders and Nauruans have been employed to an increasing extent.

The natives are a very happy, easy-going type of people, and their chief recreation is football. The Nauru team plays matches against teams of other islanders to the accompaniment of spirited barracking from the spectators. Main social attraction on the island, nevertheless, is the movies. The 4,000 inhabitants of Nauru are divided into three separate groups for film-viewing. The Europeans (who comprise about 400 of the population) go on Wednesdays and Saturdays; the Chinese (about 700) attend on Mondays and Thursdays; and the Nauruans (some 2,500) make Tuesdays and Fridays their movie nights. The remaining inhabitants — other Pacific islanders — fit in as best they can.

There is no law about this, and no one would be prevented from attending on any particular evening; it is simply that the Nauruans like to adhere to a firmly established custom. However, an absolute 'must' at the open-air movies is to bring your own seat — usually a canvas camping stool. No seats are provided, nor any shelter. If it rains, the Europeans race for their cars.

Although there are not many cars on the island there are probably more motor cycles on Nauru per head of population than anywhere else in the world. Certainly in no other country would you see so many womenfolk on motor cycles. Apart from the latter the islanders are well equipped with transistor radios, musical instruments, refrigerators and sewing machines. Hunger and poverty are unknown on Nauru with its social services and full employment. There are not enough Nauruans to mine the phosphate so other workers have to be brought in from neighbouring islands; some are brought from Hong Kong. There is no income tax, and hospital service, medical attention, electricity, water, even the movies are all free.

There is an efficient public transport service using 10 buses, and nine excellent schools provide separate education for European and native children. Outside school hours all the children play happily together and the friendly people of this island are 100 per cent literate. Well-built homes are much in evidence, and there are three hospitals — one for each race.

The Nauruans themselves are of fine physique, although not tall, and most are brown-skinned with thick black hair. They are an intelligent, Christian people who never were cannibals and although related to the Polynesians have an unknown origin. There are both Catholic and Protestant missions on the island. Except for small areas owned by the administration, the British Phosphate Commissioners, and the missions, the whole island is owned by the islanders under their traditional system of land tenure. Royalties on phosphate produced from their property are paid to the Nauruans and the only tax levied is a small annual capitation tax. The royalties give them a higher standard of living than inhabitants of other small Pacific islands could look forward to.

With the phosphate deposits estimated to peter out within 30 years, the Federal Government of Australia is planning to move the Nauruans from their island and re-settle them elsewhere. The phosphate excavations have denuded the soil of any value and the barren land will not be able to support its native population. Whether the people will be resettled on another island or in a modern village near one of the Australian capital cities, or whether they will be scattered in different places, is undecided. Mr R. Marsh, a former administrator of the Northern Territory who has been appointed to the planning task, is faced with one of the most delicate and perplexing social and adminis-tration problems ever given to a Government employee. No matter what the decision, there will be opposition. Nevertheless, Mr Marsh is determined to decide on a re-settlement plan suitable to the majority of the islanders.

The Federal Government would like to scatter the Nauruans throughout the Australian community — not settle them in a special 'Nauruan quarter' attached to a city. But it seems the Nauruans want to stay together and so retain their individuality as a people, their culture and way of life intact. They prefer the communal life they follow now in Nauru. This is understandable and the obvious answer would seem to be merely a transfer to another island. It is not as easy as all that for, undoubtedly, many things have to be taken into consideration.

There are islands available but they are generally very isolated (Nauruans are not as isolated as many other islanders in the South Seas, because of the regular, comfortable and cheap passages to Australia and New Zealand on the phosphate ships), and would not be able to support a population of nearly 2,500 in a manner to give the islanders the prosperity they enjoy. The Nauruan community has a 'long term investment fund' into which a shilling is paid for every ton of phosphate shipped. The money is invested on behalf of the islanders until the year 2000. At present it contains more than £1½ million.

It must be remembered, too, that because of their educational opportunities and their long experience with a cash economy, the average Nauruan would not be content to be dumped on a South Sea island to live a back-to-nature existence. He has his basic wage plus dependance allowance for his children under the age of 16, together with many social service benefits. For his children he wants higher education, so they may enter skilled occupations and the professions. The Nauruan has full adult suffrage and is familiar with the Australian democratic system. He has his own local Government Council, with powers to make decisions — a head chief presides over 14 district chiefs in this Council — but overriding authority is vested in the Australian Administrator.

Whatever the destiny of the Nauruans, the final say on the shape of the resettlement plan rests with Australia, subject to the approval of the United Nations. At least one nation does not appreciate the sterling work of the Australian Government. In June 1963 the Russians in the United Nations Trusteeship Council asserted (probably with their tongues in their cheeks) that Australia was giving a raw deal to the Nauruans. Such unfounded criticism is utter nonsense. Australia is treating with the utmost consideration and generosity the 2,500 Nauruans who will have to be resettled before the phosphate deposits run out around the 1990s.

It is true that Australia, with Britain and New Zealand, has profited from the phosphate wealth, but without exploitation the deposits would have been of no real value to the islanders, who owe their considerable prosperity to the royalties paid them. Moreover, it was Australia who brought the Nauruans back after the war and rehabilitated the island's economy. A United Nations survey reveals that based on income per head of population Nauruans are second highest in the world, with £800 a year. Americans (£1,100) are first. Australians have only £600.

A suggested place for their new home was Curtis Island, off the Queensland coast. Their leaders are reasonably happy about this plan, as they well should be. Curtis has many advantages not offered by their own equatorial island. The only complaint made by Chief Hammer de Roburt in the Trusteeship Council was that full sovereignty was not being conceded. The Soviet delegate solemnly backed this claim.

The idea that Australia should create a 'sovereign nation', with a population no bigger than that of a country town, on an island within sight of the mainland, is preposterous. Australians are not surrendering the title to or control over any of her territory. The Nauruans will have the right to manage their local affairs. For the rest, they should be grateful for what is being offered them. Many a derelict mining community in Australia would have been glad to be treated half as well.

Curtis Island, the suggested future home for the people of Nauru, is twenty-five miles long and approximately one hundred and seventy-five square miles in area. It lies north of Gladstone and forms the eastern side of Port Curtis. Cape Capricorn, named by Captain Cook because of its nearness to the Tropic of Capricorn, is at the northern end of the island. A lighthouse some thirty feet high stands on the summit, and there is another lighthouse — a pilot station — at Sea Hill.

There are two cattle stations on Curtis Island, the main part of which consists of high sandhills on which grow wattle trees and much scrub. The island is a good fishing area with whiting in abundance; small crabs are used chiefly for bait. Some of the families on Curtis have large oyster leases and are kept very busy attending them. The children receive their school lessons by correspondence from Brisbane, as do many others on Queensland islands.

148

19

The Unexpected Island

NORFOLK ISLAND is a personality known to too few. It is an island with a separate existence, a separate soul, a place of things distinctive from all else in these Australian islands. Little altered from the time when Captain James Cook sailing in the *Resolution* sighted it in 1774 and made a landing there, everything about the island is unexpected. Great basalt cliffs dip sharply to the ocean with the famous Norfolk Island pines presenting a backdrop not seen anywhere else in the South Seas. Elsewhere, vivid green hills undulate down to beaches of water-worn stones, where the breakers froth as they ceaselessly rush to engulf the shore. Lazy lanes wind aimlessly between tall unruly clumps of hibiscus, frangipanni and bouganvillea blooms. Myriads of red and yellow guavas of luscious flavour grow everywhere; so, too, do the wild bush lemons. Much of the countryside is reminiscent of old England, but always the mighty Norfolk pines, at heights of 150 feet, dominate the landscape. Always, too, the air is rich with the tang of the Pacific, whether one is exploring the hilltop fastnesses that seem so remote and isolated or watching the spirited little streams leaping and whirling and making endless music in their hurry to the sea.

The island is of volcanic origin similar to that of Lord Howe Island. The equable climate has a temperature range of 49-85 degrees F. and an average annual rainfall of 53 inches, evenly distributed throughout the year. Apart from those fruits growing wild on the island, cultivated varieties including bananas, oranges, figs, pineapples and passionfruit flourish abundantly. They do not appear to receive much attention, and this seems to apply to most things there. Excessive labour is required of no one. No high cost of living or expensive amusements, beyond a weekly movie, disturbs Norfolk's sylvan meditations. The chief responsibility is that men between the ages of 21 and 55 must contribute nine days' labour a year, or pay roughly £3 tax. The labouring chore is a little light work on road maintenance; everyone makes a picnic of it, with other members of the family joining in the outing.

Norfolk is compact, measures five miles by three miles, and has an area of about 8,500 acres. It has two uninhabited islands as neighbours: Nepean Island, a small limestone formation, is about half a mile distant; and Phillip Island, of decomposed basalt, rising to a height of about 900 feet, is three miles distant. Approached by air from the south, Norfolk appears as a sea-girded well-wooded park. Grassy slopes and valleys are studded profusely with the famed giant Norfolk Island pines and oak trees.

Every islander turns out fortnightly on consecutive Saturdays and Sundays to greet incoming airliners from Sydney and Auckland. The airport alongside the modern airfield near Kingston is a social centre and clearing house for island gossip and news. Time to the Islanders is regulated by these arrivals. Rather than saying, 'Come and see me next Tuesday', they say, 'Come and see me Tuesday after (or before) plane day'.

Some 60 kinds of birds are found on the island, the breeding land-birds numbering about 20 species. The twin peaks of Mount Pitt (1,039 ft.) were at one time the breeding ground of the brown-headed petrel, or mutton-bird. Many thousands of these aptly-called 'birds of providence' were taken for food by the starving early settlers until eventually the species became extinct on the island. In August 1790 Lieutenant Ralph Clark wrote from Norfolk Island: 'The Mount Pitt birds have been the greatest friends that any of us ever knew, for . . . the greatest part of us would have been in our graves long ago if it had not been for these

The Metropolitan Islands of Sydney, photographed from 32,000 feet

Phillip Island, seen through the famous pines on Norfolk Island, 900 miles North East of Sydney

birds . . . they are nearly all gone; they just lasted until the arrival of the supply ships.'

It was the towering pines of once uninhabited Norfolk that first attracted England's interest after the island was discovered in 1774 by Captain Cook. It was thought the timber would be valuable in masts for British sailing ships, and that the flax growing wild in the valleys could serve for canvas. Knots in the pines, however, made this wood unsuitable and the flax was insufficient in quantity. So Norfolk became, because of its fertility, a British convict settlement which was used to produce grain to supply other Pacific penal colonies. In 1793 the island's yield was 12,000 bushels of wheat and 50 tons of potatoes.

Norfolk Island pines live to great ages. Sydney possessed a famous one which became known as 'The Wishing Tree'. It stood for about 130 years in the Botanic Gardens after being transplanted from the garden of Mrs Macquarie (whose husband was Governor during 1810-21). The tree had outgrown Mrs Macquarie's garden and continued to flourish in its new location. The pine eventually decayed with age and in 1945 a new Wishing Tree was planted.

Out there in the South Pacific, hundreds of miles from telephones and traffic, Norfolk is really out of this world. Here in these bountiful blue waters are most of the fish you know and a lot of Norfolk's own (Big Eye, Ofi, Yahooli, and Tweed Trousers are some). King Fish, Trumpeter, Hapuka, Mackerel, Garfish, Trevally, Groper and Whiting — Tuna, too. 'Put down a line with eight hooks,' the islanders say, 'and if you only pull up seven fish, they're not biting!'

Nowhere around Norfolk is there a haven for ships. This lack has been a severe handicap to the island, but there also lies the root of its fascination, that indefinite hypnotism that the island exerts upon the stranger. For, in a world of strain and anxiety, life on Norfolk remains unhurried and peaceful. Here time stands still. There is scarcely a sound except the chattering of birds and the occasional purring of a motor vehicle or a horse trotting by. The island has no newspaper, there is only a part-time telephone service, the residents pay no income tax and goods are duty free. Mercifully there has been little or no tourist 'development' and Norfolk makes no claims to chromium-plated retreats for tired tycoons, or naïve imitations of Las Vegas or Miami. One modest hotel and a few small but well-run guest houses cater for visitors, most of whom seem to go there primarily to buy duty-free goods. I must admit that I also took advantage of such bargain buying and purchased a camera for £19 which was £15 less than the price in Sydney. There are but two modern shops (I'm speaking of my 1962 visit), the few others being quaint outback-type stores, ill-lit (indeed, almost in darkness), and with a curious conglomeration of goods in haphazard display. Peppermints, post-cards, hairpins, marbles, tea towels and toffee side by side. Stepping into one of these little stores is like stepping back into the nineteenth century, and the illusion is complete when you are served by an elderly proprietor looking like a character from a Dickens novel.

Norfolk is 900 miles from Sydney, or five hours flying time. You can also get there aboard the *Tulagi* from Sydney, taking five days, but the *Tulagi* makes a six weeks' trip to northern groups, too, and has passenger accommodation only for twelve. Moreover, the vessel has to anchor well off the island and the often choppy sea makes passenger transference by lighter a formidable mal-de-mer test.

By air is the best way to visit the island, and the five hours pass all too quickly with the luxurious treatment afforded by Qantas. Scarcely has the plane left the ground before preliminaries begin to what seems a non-stop orgy of eating. The menu cards with their distinctive Australian motifs rival those of overseas liners, and even have a page for autographs — but how and why passengers collect autographs on a five hours' plane trip I do not know. There are hot and cold savouries from Devils on Horseback to Caviar and Pate de foie Gras. Great platters of cheese of many types and baskets of choice fruit are brought round after a banquet-like meal of seafood, chicken champeaux, tossed salads, and other courses. Most remarkable of all, drinks are 'on the house': martini, moselle, burgundy, or if you prefer, just plain beer, followed by liqueurs with your coffee. Happy landing is assured after such lavish service.

My visit to Norfolk Island was not only to survey its charms but to see what the years had done to its double heritage as a one-time infamous penal colony and a home for descendants of the storied *Bounty* mutineers. Today even more progeny of those defiant British seamen and their Tahitian wives live on this island than on lonely Pitcairn, their original home. Norfolk's population of about one thousand are mostly descendants of the *Bounty* mutineers, who were brought from Pitcairn Island in 1856. They are known locally as Islanders, while the settlers and officials from Australia and New Zealand are referred to as Mainlanders.

Beautiful as the island is, nevertheless, first sight of the ruins of the convict settlement produces mixed feelings. From nearby Nepean Island's quarries came sombre grey stone for the prisons and barracks whose ruins are still grim reminders of the human misery that once prevailed in the dreaded island of no escape. This glorious garden of the ocean, so peaceful, serene and dignified, resounded with the shrieks of prisoners writhing beneath the lash. No greater contrast could be imagined than the diabolical discipline in a region where nature has spread her gentlest, sweetest charms.

The Commonwealth Government deserves praise for its decision to spend £20,000 on preserving and restoring some of the old convict relics. It was a tragedy when the early Pitcairners set fire to the settlements and tried to wipe out the relics. It is all very well for Norfolk Islanders to say 'Let us forget about the bad days'. If ever we have an opportunity to remember how inhuman were the rulers of the British Empire not much more than a hundred years ago, we have only to go to Norfolk Island to see the evidence.

Walls of the convict buildings complete with stone turrets and gun slots are surprisingly solid. Gallows Gate and several other gateways of interesting architectural design are well preserved. It was through Gallows Gate that the convicts came on their last march to meet the hangman. One can still see the indentations of the thirteen steps which they mounted to the gallows.

All the convict buildings, whether in ruins or otherwise, are located in the so-called 'capital' of the island — Kingston. This is a very beautiful site, but it must be unique among capitals. Kingston has a population of only twenty-one people, mainly government officials and clerks. And there isn't a single shop. Along the main street — Quality Row — are some well-preserved and handsome buildings such as the three-storied barracks (now the court-house), the first Government House and the guard-house. Also an elaborate below-ground stone enclosure with steps leading to the Officers' Bath, still with its freshwater stream. My curiosity was aroused at seeing local residents coming out of the guard-house carrying supplies of grog. Poking my head into the doorway I saw a counter behind which were shelves well stocked with wines, spirits and beer. A barman was wrapping up bottles for a customer. But there was no name of a licensee over the doorway nor any notice to the effect of being licensed to sell spirituous liquors. The original occupants of the guard-house would have been surprised to learn of its present function.

It was in Quality Row where lived the garrison officers in fine colonial style. Some of their homes of carved rock are used as administrative quarters of Norfolk Island officials. These buildings and ruins in Quality Row and elsewhere bear clearly-marked names. They include the hated crankmill where chained convicts trod the mill to grind corn; officers' quarters, the Catholic and Protestant churches, the little cottage where William Charles Wentworth was born, the salt mill and the blacksmiths' shops. Housing two thousand convicts, as well as all the warders, military and officials, the penal settlement at Norfolk Island was a very much bigger colony than that of Tasmania's Port Arthur.

Close to the main convict buildings is the cemetery, still in use. The lower portion is the burial ground of many convicts, soldiers and officials; the rest of the cemetery holds the bodies of early Pitcairners and residents of later years. Prisoners executed for rebellion are buried in unhallowed ground outside the cemetery. Crude headstones, roughly inscribed, and marking the graves of other convicts who were hanged may be seen inside the cemetery. Apparently they were placed there by fellow convicts. Some of those who died by the hangman were barely out of their 'teens. One headstone reveals that a convict who died at the great age of 105 was given one hundred lashes at the age of 90 for trouble-making.

You can see also the tombstone of the two soldiers who lost their lives from Barney Duffy's curse. Barney Duffy was an escaped prisoner who lived on the island undiscovered for seven years. The officials thought that he must have been drowned, but Barney had made his home in a tree in a heavily-wooded part of the island. How he managed about food is unknown, but perhaps some of the convicts may have left scraps of food for him in a secret place. At any rate, when two soldiers unexpectedly discovered Barney his hair and beard were nearly down to his waist. They cornered the runaway and brought him back to the settlement where he was promptly sentenced to be hanged. On the scaffold, Barney Duffy cursed the two soldiers responsible for his capture, and by a strange coincidence both men were drowned the following day when their boat upturned.

The oldest tombstone is erected over the grave of Thomas Headington and records that he died in 1798 at the age of 40. The epitaph is a relatively cheerful one, scorning rhythm in its verse:

> Dear wife do not grieve
> Nor children shed a tear
> For I am gone to Heaven above
> To meet sweet angels there.

An intriguing epitaph is that on the tombstone of convict James Saye:

> Christian, stop and meditate
> On this man's sad and awful fate

On earth no more he breathes again
He lied in hope and died in pain.

The explanation for the puzzling last line is that he lied to save himself from punishment for some misdeed, but to no avail. Ordered 100 lashes he collapsed and died after 56 strokes.

Many are the headstones over the graves of young Irishmen, and their epitaphs often reveal a spirit of mateship:

Farewell dear comrades and long farewell
I am doomed no more on earth to dwell
Whose time on earth will not be long
For, like a lily fresh and green,
I am cut down and no more seen.

*   *   *

Come all ye comrades standing by
As you are now so once was I
As I am now so you must be
Prepare for death and follow me.

One tombstone records that the deceased, Stephen Smith, was 'murdered by a body of prisoners on the 1st July 1846 whilst in the execution of his duty at the settlement cookhouse.' Some may wonder whether his sad fate had any connection with his culinary efforts. A matter of speculation, too, concerns the person 'who became the untimely victim of a disease produced by a trifling accident.'

At least one lady is recorded as having attained her musical ambition:

To sing God's praises was her desire
And now she's gone to join the heavenly choir.

A few yards from the cemetery in a beautiful vale is a well-proportioned stone bridge crossing a stream. Known as Bloody Bridge, its story is a grim one. Prisoners building the bridge slew their guard and when they saw a group of soldiers approaching they concealed the body in the masonry and continued laying the stonework. When the soldiers reached them they said that the guard had fallen into the stream and been quickly washed out to sea. The soldiers could not disprove the story but just as they were walking away one of them saw a trickle of blood seeping through the masonry. Needless to say, the convicts were all hanged and their bodies buried in unhallowed ground outside the cemetery.

The first colonization of the island was undertaken in 1788, when Governor Arthur Phillip of the new colony of New South Wales sent Lieutenant P. G. King in H.M.S. *Supply* to take possession of the island and to establish a small penal station as a branch of the settlement at Port Jackson. In 1813 because of administrative expenses and the difficulties of maintaining communications the station was abandoned. During those first twenty-five years conditions at the convict station were satisfactory and prisoners received fair treatment. Thirteen years later — in 1813 — the penal settlement was re-established on a very large scale and maintained for twenty-nine years under a brutal system that was truly horrifying.

Ten years before the penal settlement was abolished, Norfolk Island had been annexed to Van Diemen's Land, as Tasmania was then called, and it was to there that the prisoners were transferred in 1855. The all but deserted island did not remain thus for long. The following year — 1856 — Norfolk Island entered the second phase of its strange history. Three thousand seven hundred and fifty miles to the east of Norfolk lies Pitcairn Island, a tiny rocky outpost, the home of the former *Bounty* mutineers and their Tahitian wives. Pitcairn was no longer productive enough to support the growing colony and the British Government offered to transfer the settlers to Norfolk Island.

As a result, 194 Pitcairners (men, women and children) sailed for their new home. On the Government's orders there had been left on Norfolk Island for their use 2,000 sheep, 350 head of cattle, some 500 pigs, 20 horses and large quantities of preserved food and grain. Moreover, the Pitcairners were allowed to use the splendid stone government buildings, and each family was given an allotment of 50 acres of land.

The new site was a Garden of Eden compared with wild,

rugged Pitcairn, and the luxury of buildings and extensive livestock were an extra bonus. But human nature being what it is, in spite of all that was done for them many of the settlers pined for their old surroundings. They complained that Norfolk was too big an island and that the convict relics offended their religious outlook; moreover, they proceeded to burn down such reminders. Eventually 46 of the newcomers returned to their barren little island, Pitcairn. The rest remained on Norfolk, and to the community was subsequently added some British migrants and a few Australians and New Zealanders down the years. But the customs and the simple form of government evolved by the Pitcairners continued.

The last of the original Pitcairners, Mrs Marianne Selina Buffet, died on Norfolk in March 1943, aged 87 years. Practically everybody on the island is related to one another and invariably anyone you meet there will have one of seven surnames. That person is sure to be either a Quintal, Christian, Adams, McCoy, Young, Buffett or Evans. The first five names are all descended from the *Bounty* mutineers and their Tahitian women. The other two — Buffett and Evans — although descended from Pitcairners, did not arrive on Pitcairn until after the mutiny.

There are very few relics of the *Bounty* to be seen today on Norfolk Island. Outstanding are two oak planks from the ship on which are carved the Ten Commandments. The carving was done by the last survivor of the mutineers, John Adams. His real name was Alexander Smith and he was the only mutineer to survive the bitter quarrelling and bloodshed of the first years on Pitcairn Island. Apparently it was a case of the survival of the fittest, and Smith-cum-Adams must have been a ruthless old reprobate. At any rate, as he advanced in years and his family increased considerably, he became deeply religious in a unique fashion and laid down his own religious and moral laws for the future of the little community. In later years a Seventh Day Adventist missionary visited Pitcairn and today all those on Pitcairn belong to that religion.

Two other interesting *Bounty* relics to be seen on Norfolk are a large copper kettle and a china mug. The kettle, which is kept in the administrative building, was taken from the *Bounty* by William McCoy and he used it on Pitcairn for distilling alcohol made from the roots of a native plant. McCoy had once worked in a Scottish distillery and the brew he concocted in this big copper kettle was so potent that it was capable of keeping an imbiber drunk for days on end. In April 1798, its brewer went into the D.T.'s, and during one fit tied a stone around his neck and jumped into the sea. The china mug is owned by Charles Adams and has been handed down from his ancestor, one of the mutineers.

The popular image of those mutineers is that they were in the right and Captain Bligh was the villain of the piece. There is no doubt that Bligh had a caustic tongue and a ready temper. He drove his men and was impatient with inefficiency. But the records prove that he used the cat-o'-nine tails less than many other commanders of his day and he was solicitous of the welfare of his men. In dirty weather off Cape Horn he kept a fire going below, and he even gave up his own cabin to the men who had wet berths. Most remarkable, he brought them through the long voyage without a single case of scurvy.

Christian seems to have been over-sensitive — today he might be called neurotic — and given to a persecution complex. Like Bligh, he had a quick temper. It seems evident that the unpremeditated mutiny arose from a sudden impulse on the part of Christian, who smarted under Bligh's strictness. But the opportunity was quickly welcomed by the others as a chance to return to an island paradise.

Here is what Bligh had to say about it: 'I can only conjecture that the mutineers had assured themselves of a more happy life among the Otaheiteans than they could possibly have in England. The women at Otaheite are handsome, mild and cheerful . . . The chiefs were so much attached to our people that they made them promises of large possessions. Thus the mutineers imagined it in their power to fix themselves in the midst of plenty, on the finest island in the world, where they need not labour, and where the allurements of dissipation are beyond anything that can be conceived.'

We cannot hear Fletcher Christian's comments since he left no written statement about the mutiny or anything else. He realized that the authorities would search for the mutineers, hence with eight of his fellows and nineteen Polynesians he wisely left Tahiti and came to Pitcairn Island. There the strange community lived for eighteen years until an American ship called there and found only one of the original mutineers alive — Alexander Smith, who had assumed the name of John Adams. There were, of course, descendants of the others and their Tahitian womenfolk.

What happened to Fletcher Christian? To this day there is no real certainty as to what became of him, but there is evidence that he did not die on Pitcairn. His grave was the only one that John Adams could not locate when he recounted the fate of the *Bounty* mutineers to the captain of the American ship *Topaz* which called at Pitcairn in 1808.

A very interesting sidelight on the mystery is an account written by Sir John Barros who was at one time Secretary to the Admiralty. He states that about 1809 a report prevailed in Cumberland, in the neighbourhood of his native place, that Fletcher Christian had returned home. Neighbours said that he made frequent visits to a relative there and that he was living in concealment in some part of England.

That same year, according to Sir John, a singular incident occurred. Captain Heywood, whilst at Plymouth, getting his ship fitted out, happened to be passing down Fore Street when a man of unusual stature, very much muffled and with his hat drawn close over his eyes, emerged suddenly from a small side street and walked quickly past him. The height, athletic figure, and gait so impressed Heywood as being those of Christian that, quickening his pace till he came up with the stranger, he said in a tone of voice only loud enough to be heard by him, 'Fletcher Christian!' The man turned quickly round and faced his interrogator, but little of his face was visible and, darting up one of the small streets, he vanished from the other's sight. Captain Heywood hesitated for a moment, but decided on not going further into the matter.

Was it really Fletcher Christian? No one will ever know. However, whatever his end, his name is legend, and his descendants are living today in Australia, Pitcairn and Norfolk Island. Moreover, the first born son of each new generation is traditionally christened Fletcher Christian.

On Norfolk Island I spoke to and visited the homes of descendants of those who migrated from Pitcairn. One was Ike Christian, a fourth generation descendant from Fletcher Christian, and now in his eighties. The broad features and golden-olive skin tones of many Norfolk Island people reflect their partly Tahitian background. Unlike those on Pitcairn who have remained isolated, the Norfolk Islanders keep in touch with Australia and New Zealand and they have intermingled with settlers from there. They speak English with very little accent but in their own homes or whenever they are talking to each other they use a dialect brought by their ancestors from Pitcairn — a curious mixture of old west-country English and Tahitian. For example, the words Very Good: they say 'Ess goodun.' I'll go: 'I gwen.' I'm glad you came to see us: 'I glade you's a'come to see ucklun.' Their word for tomorrow is 'morla' and bananas they call 'plun'.

Some of the islanders said to me laughingly, 'Oh, we're descended from a bad lot!' but they are really proud to be descended from the mutineers who had the courage — in their opinion — to defy a captain they considered an insufferable tyrant.

An annual event is Bounty Day — June 8 — commemorating the arrival of the Pitcairners on Norfolk Island in 1856. There is always a procession of descendants dressed in naval uniforms of those times. They parade to the cemetery and then to Government House where sacred songs are sung. A big picnic follows. The islanders spread tablecloths end to end along a wall of the old convict barracks and sit on the grass, feasting on mountains of island specialities. Tahitian cookery, a heritage of the mutineers' wives, flavours

161

the menus. A typical dish is Pilhi — sweet potatoes grated and the pulp baked in a pan lined with banana leaves. This is served with products of Norfolk's rich soil such as chilli peppers, deliciosas, bananas and tomatoes. Bounty Day concludes with a cricket match — Bounty versus All-comers.

A document of importance in the history of Norfolk Island turned up in 1963 in a collection of papers at the Auckland Institute and Museum Library. Many historians doubted its existence. Dated June 25, 1856, it transferred the ownership of Norfolk Island, except certain land and buildings to be retained by the Crown, to *Bounty* mutiny descendants from Pitcairn Island.

The document was written at sea by Captain Fremantle, master of H.M.S. *Juno,* who landed on Norfolk Island soon after the Pitcairn islanders had arrived there on the vessel *Morayshire* to settle. A year earlier, he had been sent to Pitcairn Island to explain the resettlement plan. The document, addressed to the Chief Magistrate of Pitcairn Islanders on Norfolk, Mr Frederick Young, came to light in a collection of Bishop Selwyn's correspondence which had been deposited at the museum as a loan in perpetuity by the Bishop of Auckland.

There is a nine-hole golf course at Kingston, but because the island is so small the golf course also serves as pasture land. Barbed wire keeps grazing cattle from the greens, and the players enter over a stile! All the livestock are descended from cattle, sheep and pigs left on Norfolk Island for the Pitcairn colonists.

Most excellent strawberries are grown and field mushrooms are there for the picking, but Norfolk's money crop is the bean-seed. This blight-free French bean-seed is in great demand by Australian farmers. Women sort the beans best, their husbands contend, because they have nimble fingers; the men do all the field work. Some of the women can grade seven bushels a day. It may surprise many a home-gardener in Australia to know that Norfolk is almost certainly the source of the Brown Beauty, Hawkesbury Wonder, and other types of bean-seed that he grows each year.

Apart from bean-seed, there is little primary production for export.

Whaling is an important part of the island's economy. In the old days men in longboats used to go out after the hump-back whales that came north from the Antarctic in May or June to mate. When they killed a whale it took perhaps twenty hours to get it back and they always sang hymns to relieve the monotony. They would also have to wait until the tide was high to pull the whale on the beach, and as this was accomplished they sang the doxology, 'Praise God, from Whom all blessings flow!' Nowadays a motor ship with harpoon guns bags as many as 170 whales a year — a quota set up by the Commonwealth Government — and there is a modern plant at the whaling station with its winches clanking, the hiss of steam, and flensers slopping around in their high gum boots.

Norfolk Islanders themselves are among the friendliest people in the South Seas — just as long as you are not discussing politics. Norfolk's obsession with politics, during my visit there, overshadowed its other big problem — how it can earn an income of its own. It still lives on handouts from Australia, whose territory it is. As mentioned earlier, there is no income tax and very little to export. Tourism still looks the most likely possibility for the future. Now that Qantas Airways has turned its fortnightly service to Sydney into a weekly one during the summer, this is bringing an increased flow of visitors.

Just what does Norfolk Island want in the way of Government? No one seems to be in agreement. The present administrative staff is housed in the old convict buildings at Kingston. Since 1914 the island has been administered through a resident administrator appointed by the Governor-General of the Commonwealth of Australia. An advisory council, consisting of eight members and elected annually, assists the administrator. There is a chief magistrate on the island who can judge all cases except those punishable by death, for which a special court has to be constituted by the Governor-General.

Only a referendum can clear up some of the political confusion which has been baffling everybody there for so long. Small communities often become split on questions at times but Norfolk Island has for years been split wide open over the Local Government question. Side issues are many and confused and it is difficult to determine just what the Islanders are seeking in the way of future Government. However, this Pacific paradise has too much to offer to holidaymakers for them to be unduly disturbed by Norfolk's political problems.

To understand fully Norfolk and its people it has to be appreciated that the Islanders are individualists. They have their own roots, their own history, their own way of life. Exploring the island's delights on my second day there I passed a private home on the entrance gateway of which was a large notice. In letters, seemingly done by a signwriter, it read: 'No visitors between noon and 3 p.m. PLEASE.' Thinking that this must be a place open for public inspection, and since it was after three o'clock, I opened the gate and walked down the pathway to the front door. To the lady who opened it, in response to my knock, I referred to the notice and asked if there was an exhibit, or perhaps the gardens open for inspection. The lady looked astounded. 'Oh, dear, no,' she replied, 'the notice is merely for friends and tradesmen to let them know our siesta hours.'

That is Norfolk — the unexpected island.

20

'This Remarkable Little Island'

WITH its towering peaks, coral-reefed lagoon, temperate climate, dense forestal growth and abundant bird life, Lord Howe Island offers unique attractions to holiday-makers who desire to 'get away from it all'. There is something breathtaking about the first sight of Lord Howe Island when after three and a half hours' flying from Sydney the aircraft glides down on the turquoise waters of the western lagoon. Piloted by a crew of islanders in their launch, the flying-boat comes to rest at a mooring. The noise of the engines dies away, and the silence that follows seems profound. One embarks on a launch and soon approaches the pier, where many of the islanders and visitors have gathered to watch the arrival of the plane and its passengers.

Lord Howe is the most southerly island known to have coral reefs. Lying off the east coast of the New South Wales mainland, about 436 miles north-east of Sydney, the island is roughly crescent-shaped, seven miles long by up to one mile wide. Innumerable beauties of nature are packed into its restrictive boundaries — majestic mountains, fern gullies, palm groves filled with flowering shrubs and butterflies, a coral fringed lagoon, rock pools holding fish of dazzling colours, curious shells and seaweed of rich and extraordinary shades. Banyan, pandanus and other tropical trees line the gullies and lowlands, and the cliffs and adjacent islands hold countless sea-birds which, when disturbed, almost darken the sky. Lord Howe is but one of a group of 28 islands and islets — on some of which no man has set foot.

Think of that! There is still adventure for those who long to explore the unknown.

The main core of the island is composed of volcanic rock of great antiquity, but some rock was also formed by wind-blown coral. Geologists believe that both Lord Howe Island and Norfolk Island were once part of the New Zealand volcanic land-mass, to which they are still connected by deep sunken banks. This theory is supported by the existence on both the islands of many forms of flora and fauna which have marked affinities with those of New Zealand and of Polynesia generally. The layman feels that this remarkable little island has somehow in the past been mysteriously transplanted from the higher latitudes of the tropics. Its appearance is such that it suggests all the best features of the South Sea islands of romantic fiction without the stern realities of the South Sea of facts — such as exhausting climate, fevers and aggressive insects other than mosquitoes. The latter, however, are of a mild variety. No snakes are found on Lord Howe; the climate is remarkably equable, frosts are unknown, and the temperatures range between 60 and 80 degrees.

The crowning glory of the island is its vegetation. Among the noteworthy endemic plants are four species of palms, known collectively as 'Kentia palms' among nurserymen, each growing at different altitudes and unable to survive outside that particular one. The most striking tree on the island is an endemic banyan fig *(Ficus columnaris)*. Beginning life as an epiphyte in crevices of other trees, it sends down trailing stems that after a time strangle the host, and later develop adventitious roots that form rope-like stems. These secondary root-stems often coalesce to form trunks, a few dozen of which may cover an area of up to three acres. The timber is used for furniture. There are ferns and mosses on the island that occur nowhere else in the world, and the top of Mount Gower is a veritable paradise of plant life. Superb tree-ferns grow on the slopes of the mountains and a profusion of filmy ferns such as 'maidenhair' and 'adder's tongue'.

The number of bird species recorded for Lord Howe

Shrouded in mist, the impressive peaks of Lord Howe Island,
some 400 miles off the New South Wales coast

Lord Howe Islanders use these sleds for transporting goods on the Island

Island is approximately 100. One of the most interesting of the indigenous birds is the flightless woodhen which may be seen in the luxuriant vegetation of the mountain areas. Many thousands of terns, noddies, petrels, gannets and tropic-birds breed in various parts of the island or on the adjacent islets, principally the Admiralties. Rich as is its bird life, Lord Howe has lost many of its indigenous land-birds, exterminated mainly by man. Eight kinds of birds — a pigeon, the white swamphen, a parrot, a warbler, a fan-tail, the vinous-tinted blackbird, the robust silvereye, and a native starling — have become extinct. The slaughter seems to have been very great soon after the island was discovered. Knowing no enemies other than their own kind (for no predatory animals existed on the island), they fell before the sticks and stones of hungry sailors. Later, following settlement in 1834, many birds were killed for food or were shot out, as was the case with the parrot because of the damage it did to crops. Much bird life, too, was exterminated after the ill-fated day in 1918 when the S.S. *Makambo* struck an uncharted rock off Lord Howe. Rats came ashore from the stricken vessel and took refuge in the thick and tangled scrub. Beset by no natural enemies they multiplied with great rapidity living on birds' eggs and doing untold damage to the crops.

Towering far above the rest of the island are two great peaks — Mount Gower (2,840 feet) and Mount Lidgbird (2,504 feet). Like two guardian citadels (and more impressive than Waikiki's famed Diamond Head) they provide an endless source of fascination as they collect and then impale the clouds that are attracted to their summits. Around the base of these mountains, where the island reaches its scenic triumph, pandanus and palm forests close in with jungle-like thickness. Separating the two peaks is the wild and rugged Erskine Valley.

Ten miles to the south-east stands an extraordinary triangular pillar of rock rising 1,816 feet sheer from the ocean. Known as Ball's Pyramid, the rock is the nesting-place of countless sea-birds. The water surrounding it is crystal clear and is teeming with fish of all kinds. It would be hard to equal this fishing ground anywhere else in the world, and even the most exacting fisherman, after an hour or so, will lay down his rod or line with a sigh and admit that he has had enough. To the accompaniment of screams and shrill cries from the hundreds of terns circling your launch you land fish after fish after fish. Kingfish 20 or 30 lbs. in weight, trevalli, salmon, blue-fish, zebra-fish, and maybe a shark or two. Visitors are invited to look through a water-glass over the sides of the launch and view the depths beneath. The sight is an unforgettable one. The floor of the ocean, three or four fathoms deep, is more beautiful than the loveliest of gardens, and it seems incredible that such thousands of fish of so many varieties could gather in one spot. But not only here — all around the shores of Lord Howe could be described as a fisherman's heaven.

For many years the income of the island was derived mainly from the gathering of palm seed (the harvesting of the seeds takes place about the middle of March), but from about 1914 onwards there was a decline in the palm seed trade and it is now but a minor industry. Another all but vanished sight is that of the horse-drawn sleighs pulling loads of stores or produce. There are very few motor vehicles; most islanders have bicycles and these are very popular with visitors who hire them for £1 weekly.

The island was discovered by Lieutenant Henry Lidgbird Ball, commander of H.M.Tender *Supply* during a voyage from Port Jackson to Norfolk Island in 1788. It was named after Richard Howe, the famous British admiral. Since there was no game and no good anchorage, the island was neglected for many years after its discovery. In 1834 a small settlement was formed from New South Wales under the leadership of two partners named Dawson and Poole. (No traces have been found of any previous occupation by natives.) Dawson found the venture unprofitable and departed, leaving Poole in charge and who for many years ruled the island in patriarchal fashion. By 1851 the settlement consisted of 16 persons who had become virtually self-subsistent. Some revenue was obtained from the supplying of provisions to the many whalers calling at the island.

As the result of development of an export trade in the seed of the Kentia (or Howea) palm to many parts of the world, the population had reached 100 early in the present century.

Two of the earliest settlers on the island were Alan Moseley and his wife, Johanna, who commenced their long residence in 1843. Their arrival was most romantic, if unorthodox. Alan was the navigating officer of a whaling ship that called at Sydney Town. There he met and fell in love with Johanna. She was equally a target for Cupid's dart; so much so that she could not bear the thought of saying goodbye to her lover on his long voyage to foreign lands. As a result, Alan contrived to smuggle his sweetheart aboard his ship in a packing case.

Soon after the vessel left Sydney the Captain discovered the stowaway. Furious, he swore that he would dump Johanna ashore on the first bit of land the ship sighted — even if it happened to be a desert island. Fortunately for the girl the first land they sighted was Lord Howe Island, and put ashore she was. All ended happily, however, when eventually Alan finished his long voyage and managed to return to the island where Johanna was pining for him. An ex-captain married them there; it being the first marriage ceremony on Lord Howe. Fifty years later they learned that their marriage by the ex-mariner had not been legal, so the old couple went through another marriage ceremony to make matters right. When reading the inscriptions on their tombstones in a little cemetery near 'Pine Trees' guest-house, I noticed that Alan died at the age of 89 and Johanna lived to be 97.

Of the island's silvery scimitar-shaped beaches one of the most popular is Ned's Beach, with its dense palm glade that steals down to the sands. From this beach there is a magnificent view of the Admiralty Islets. The surfing beach known as Blinkies is a truly lovely one with a crystal-clear rock pool at the northern end. Overlooking a little bay called Slyph's Hole two lone pines rise as a memorial to one of Lord Howe's few shipping disasters. The twin pines grow as monuments to a broken heart and a lost love.

The tragic episode occurred in 1873 when the islanders'

ketch, *Slyph*, sailed for Sydney laden with produce and passengers. A husband of a young woman who, with their two children, was aboard the vessel, farewelled his family and then from between the pines uneasily watched the *Slyph* fade over the horizon. The ketch never reached Sydney; caught in a gale, it was lost with all hands. For months afterwards the distraught husband, refusing to recognize his loss, daily came down to the pines and searched the seas in vain for some sign of the missing *Slyph*. Broken-hearted, he did not long survive his tragedy. Before he died he expressed a wish that he should be buried under the pines where he had last seen his family depart. His wish was respected. Today the lone pines at the little bay are giants, a conspicuous landmark along that part of the coast. But few visitors know their sad history.

Mount Gower boasts a tale of treasure trove. It began when the whaling brig *George* ran short of water and put in at Lord Howe in 1830. As she approached she struck a rock in a deep bay and foundered. The vessel carried bullion to the extent of 5,000 sovereigns, the result of a previous successful expedition, and before it sank the captain managed to remove the precious cargo ashore. Believing the island to be inhabited by wild natives, the castaways buried their treasure at a particular spot near the south base of the mountain.

Eventually they were rescued by another whaling vessel which also put in for water. Not wishing to disclose the whereabouts of the bullion to his rescuers, the captain decided to leave the treasure temporarily behind. The following year he and his men found an opportunity to return to the island. To their astonishment and dismay they found that during their absence the entire shape of the bay had changed; an immense landslide had avalanched down, completely burying under thousands of tons of basalt rock the site where the bullion had been deposited.

Landslides are by no means uncommon on the precipitous faces of Mount Gower and its neighbour Mount Lidgbird; many a one has torn down from the heights since that fateful one. The exact spot being unknown where the treasure lies buried, but the known knowledge of the hopeless task, there has never been a treasure-seeking expedition organized to retrieve Lord Howe's lost riches.

Lord Howe Island is extraordinarily law-abiding, and consequently lacks gaol and policeman. True, it once possessed a lock-up but from the day of its erection until its demolition half a century later not a soul was imprisoned in it. No wonder that when it was first sent there by the New South Wales Government the islanders refused to land it. What did they want with a lock-up?

Admittedly, one person had been imprisoned before the advent of the lock-up. In 1873 a deserter from a whaleboat, a man named Moss, made his way to the island. Because he refused to do any work, the residents chained him to a tree. One night he escaped, took to the mountains, and threatened to burn down the houses and the store. The threat caused great consternation among the inhabitants, and in consequence the buildings were surrounded by casks of water as a precaution. Moreover, a watch was kept night and day. Fortunately the escapee was soon captured.

The inhabitants made sure that the lazy scoundrel would not get away a second time. Stocks were constructed to hold him — the old English type consisting of a wooden frame with holes in it for the head, hands and feet. The more tender-hearted islanders suggested that this type of punishment might cause him to become a cripple, so another mode of captivity was adopted. The villain was put into a large cask and headed up in it. There was just a small trapdoor cut into one side of the cask which allowed food and drink to be passed into the prisoner. He could adopt only two positions — either stand up or lie down. The inhabitants were taking no chances, and determined to keep the culprit in the cask until he could be taken to Sydney on the next ship that called there. It was some months before a Sydney-bound vessel called to Lord Howe Island. The prisoner was taken aboard, still in the cask, and landed thus in Sydney.

The island possesses no street lighting, no telephones (although there are both radio and cable communications

with Australia), and no hotels. The permanent population
is about 200 and tourists number about the same or more,
depending on the time of year. The islanders are a white-
skinned race. Cradled by the encircling sea and forever
enveloped in the timeless crashing tumult of sound from
the surf, it is not surprising that the hardy inhabitants
should be descendants of early whalers and seamen. A few
families show traces of a Maori ancestry, of which they are
justly proud. Three New Zealanders and their Maori wives,
together with two children were among the very first settlers.

Constitutionally, Lord Howe Island is part of New South
Wales and is included in the State electorate of King and
in the Commonwealth electorate of West Sydney. There
is an Island Committee which consists of four members
elected by the islanders. The power and functions of this
Committee are to make recommendations to the Board of
Control in Sydney on matters relating to the island and
its affairs and to exercise any power or duty which it is
authorized by the Board to perform. No outsider is allowed
to become a permanent member of the community unless
he marries a Lord Howe Islander and has lived there for
a period of 10 years. A most necessary condition, also, is a
record of good behaviour and unblemished character.

Lord Howe has been in the news of late years because
the Woollahra Council of Sydney wants to have the Rose
Bay flying-boat base closed. If the base goes, Lord Howe
Island will be deprived of air transport. There is no aerodrome for land-based planes and the islanders have mixed
feelings about the Civil Aviation Department's vague pro-
posals to build one — some day. They want a good air service, but a landing strip would absorb a considerable part
of the island's level and arable surface. Much of Lord Howe's
charm lies in its rich vegetation and peaceful atmosphere.
Construction of an aerodrome would change its whole
character. Yet without one sooner or later it will be cut
off from the mainland, with a subsequent loss of the tourist
trade on which most of the islanders subsist. The answer may
lie in present developments of planes that require only
short runways for taking-off and landing.

A holiday on Lord Howe can be less expensive than many an interstate one. During my visit in March, 1964, I stayed at a guest-house whose modest tariff of seventeen guineas a week covered not only all meals and accommodation but morning and afternoon teas and supper as well. On the weekly dance night in the spacious lounge, drinks were 'on the house' — spirits, wines, beer and soft drinks. Then, too, there was the buffet dinner with the tables arranged like a wedding banquet and festooned with island blossoms. The fine foods and their variety were of luxury hotel standard. And as a prelude to the occasion drinks were again 'on the house'. Little wonder that guests return there year after year and some twice yearly. All the guest-houses have their 'regulars'; at 'Ocean View' I met two men who were making their tenth visit, another his thirteenth, and one — believe it or not — who had stayed at the same guest-house forty-eight times!

Departing visitors — men and women alike — are fare-welled near the pier with leis of freshly-picked hibiscus and frangipanni. To the accompaniment of good wishes, au revoir kisses and much banter, the lovely garlands are placed around one's neck where they remain for but a brief time. On the short launch trip to the waiting flying-ship it is traditional to cast the leis of blossoms into the translucent waters so that they may float ashore and thus ensure the granting of one's wish to return to the island.

Few can visit this tiny Australian outpost of the Pacific without gaining a lasting admiration for the grandeur of the scenery, the peace and beauty of its satellite islets, and the innate graciousness of the people who dwell on Lord Howe.

21

The Gabo Light

ABOUT 5 miles south-west of the extreme eastern tip of Victoria and separated from the mainland by a narrow shallow channel lies the small but well known Gabo Island. The island is familiar to many coastal sea travellers because of the fact that it is here where ships make the turn from the south to the east coast, and vice versa. On the north-west of the granite island, some 1¾ miles long, is a pleasant little bay with a jetty, otherwise the main point of interest is the lighthouse. The latter is a very important one for this busy shipping lane, and it exhibits two lights at an elevation of 179 feet, one for the south and the other for the east coast traffic.

There are three lighthouse families on Gabo including nine children aged from five to fifteen years. A distinctive local touch is given to Christmas celebrations. A Christmas tree is decorated but the children need to write to Santa three months beforehand, otherwise they could not be sure their orders would be received in time. On Christmas Day the three families have dinner in their own homes, but in the afternoon they have a get-together with presents for the children, a few drinks and carol singing. Christmas — and indeed any other season — is an idyllic time on Gabo Island. No traffic jams, no crowded shops, no hordes of tourists. There is an inviting sandy beach, oysters are plentiful on the rocks, and there is never a shortage of fish and crayfish.

Few of the many people on the ships that pass Gabo Island are aware that it was in these waters where the first steamer to cross the Pacific Ocean was smashed to pieces. On a sandy part of Gabo lies a heap of granite blocks almost covered with grass scrub. One block bears the inscription: THIS MONUMENT, ERECTED BY THE GOVERNMENTS OF VICTORIA AND NEW SOUTH WALES, IS IN MEMORY OF THOSE DROWNED BY THE WRECK OF THE STEAMSHIP MONUMENTAL CITY, 18TH MAY, 1853, ON TALLABERGA ISLAND, WHERE THEIR REMAINS LIE BURIED.

The memorial to the thirty-three men, women and children who perished in the wreck was originally an obelisk on a plinth. Burrowing sea-birds over the century and more weakened the foundations, and the memorial collapsed leaving the inscribed block lying flat on the sand to be overgrown with scrub. It is a monument worth preserving, and it is to be hoped that Government assistance will be forthcoming to restore it before it is entirely forgotten.

The S.S. *Monumental City,* a vessel of 1,000 tons, made her epic voyage from San Francisco to Sydney in 1853, taking 65 days for the journey. Port Jackson gave an enthusiastic welcome to the pioneer screw-steamer as she proudly steamed up the harbour on April 23 of that year. Crowds lined the foreshores and civic receptions awaited the commander and officers. Twelve days later the *Monumental City* sailed for Melbourne where her business was brief. On May 13 she left for the return voyage to America, via Sydney, with eighty passengers from Melbourne. A few of them, and some of the crew, were a little uneasy about the sailing date, and their superstitions were strengthened when the vessel narrowly avoided colliding with another ship as she cleared Port Phillip Heads. Six days later newspapers announced that the *Monumental City* was overdue, but could be expected to arrive shortly. They were not yet aware that the vessel had met her doom four days previously near Gabo Island.

Among the passengers was a retired ship's captain who had had practical experience of the hazards of the southeast coast. He warned Captain W. H. Adams, an American in command of the *Monumental City,* several times during the night before the disaster that the ship was sailing dangerously near the coast, but his advice was ignored. About four o'clock on the Sunday morning of June 4 first mate Edward Van Sice saw land looming through the heavy rain and realized that the captain had mistaken another headland for Cape Howe. He altered course on his own initiative, without calling the master who was sleeping in his cabin, and in doing so ran the vessel on to the rocks.

Awakened at feeling the strong concussion, passengers and crew hurried to the deck but the morning was dark, bleak and rain-lashed, and it was impossible to see the rocks against which the vessel had run. Daylight revealed the grim mass of rocks which held the *Monumental City* and a cauldron of seething seas, roaring and spuming at the base of the island. In the distance could be seen the hazy shoreline of the mainland.

Mr Gavin Harrow, one of the passengers, in his story published in the *Shipping Gazette* of June 4, 1853, said that it was proposed firstly to send the women passengers and children ashore, but when they saw the mountainous waves swirling around them they were frightened to leave. They remained as eye-witnesses — and later as victims — of one of the cruellest of all deaths — death in sight of land and safety. In any case it probably would have been impossible to land the women and children, for when attempts were made to launch the boats three of them were smashed in quick succession. It seemed that the infuriated sea was mad with blood-lust. Grotesque arms of water tore at the timbers as they were freed from the rigging, held them aloft, and drove them like battering rams against the side of the vessel. The noble *Monumental City* which had made Pacific history could not stand against that. She was beginning to shiver in her death-throes.

One heroic seaman, Charles Plummer, volunteered for the dangerous task of taking the sole remaining lifeboat to try to get ashore with a line. Skilfully he played the boat against the treachery of the waves and miraculously succeeded. A cheer went up from all when the hero plunged into the surf and struggled, bruised and breathless, up the beach. As soon as the line was safely fixed, the second mate volunteered to go ashore on the hawser to test its strength. He was successful but was exhausted and badly bruised. By this time the stern of the vessel began to break up and passengers and crew broke into open panic; they fought in a milling, struggling crowd to reach the bowsprit, trying to get to the hawser.

Fifty-three people managed to reach the shore by means of the hawser before an immense sea crashed down on the wreck. Men, women and children were hurled into the boiling surf strewn with timber and all kinds of wreckage. Death came with merciful swiftness; there were no prolonged struggles to harrow those who watched from the rocks. According to survivors, Captain Adams was conspicuous by his lack of heroism and disregard of the traditions of the sea. There were between 40 and 50 people still aboard the wreck when he left it, and he went ashore at least an hour before the last passenger attempted escape. It was claimed, also, that he promised to return and his failure to do so caused dismay among the women and other passengers still hoping for rescue.

On a miserable Sunday afternoon the survivors built a small fire on the beach, and sorted out their provisions which they estimated might last, with care, for sixteen days. Sunday night brought a biting wind and showers that soaked the castaways, adding to their misery. The following dawn revealed many bodies strewn along the beach, some of which were unrecognizable. A simple burial service was held before the bodies were interred in a common grave on the island which they learned later was Tallaberga, near Gabo Island.

The sea had somewhat abated by Tuesday morning so 19 men, including the captain, decided to make for the mainland. They were successful but during that run ashore the captain was alleged to have thrown two young stewards overboard to lighten the boat through the surf. Neither of them could swim and they were fortunate in being able to struggle ashore. It had been agreed that the boat would return to the island to take other castaways to the mainland but the weather looked ominous and it was decided to wait for smoother seas. When the following day brought no improvement in the weather the men decided to form a party to walk to the whaling station at Twofold Bay to obtain assistance. And so they set off through the unknown bush.

In the meantime the remainder of the survivors on the island became anxious and were eager to reach the mainland. Several of the seamen built a raft and with the sea now calm, and a sunny sky, they launched it and successfully bridged the gap between the island and the mainland. The others were also transported from the island, together with the provisions.

Seven and a half days after the *Monumental City* went to her doom near Gabo a party of the castaways staggered into the little settlement at Twofold Bay. Bearded, hungry and weary, they gasped their story and sank exhausted where they stood. Willing assistance was given them, the other castaways were rounded up, and all helped to reach Sydney.

The official inquiry concerning the wreck caused bitter controversy. Accusations were made by many survivors and some of the crew that Captain Adams was arrogant, ruthless, inefficient and cowardly. Nevertheless, the New South Wales Steam Navigation Board dismissed the charges and turned their condemnation to the hapless first mate, accusing him of being 'unofficer-like, unjustifiable, and culpable'. Captain Adams had already put the entire blame on him. The disturbing verdict led to many angry letters to Sydney and Melbourne newspapers, one of them being written by John Perry, one of the stewards the captain had thrown overboard. He said that he applied to appear as a witness at the enquiry but was not called upon, 'owing, as I am told, to the captain having the option of calling only those witnesses he pleased, as the board sat at his request.'

The triumph of the first screw-steamer to cross the Pacific, the 'magnificently fitted' *Monumental City*, was a short-lived one, but its tragic loss had one redeeming feature. It resulted in the building of the lighthouse on Gabo Island and made safe the passage of other ships along that treacherous coast where for years mariners had warned of the vital necessity for a guiding light.

22

Kangaroo Island

RISING from the Southern Ocean like some leviathan of the deep, the irregular bulk of Kangaroo Island lies off the entrance to St. Vincent's Gulf in South Australian waters. On its southern flanks the great combers of the Southern Ocean expend their energy; on its northern coastline it is fondled by the more placid waters of Investigator Strait. Approximately 90 miles long by 34 miles at its widest part, the island is the largest one off the South Australian coast, and (Tasmania excepted) the second largest in Australian waters, Melville Island, N.T., being the largest.

The coastline of Kangaroo Island is composed chiefly of steep cliffs, which at its western end reach heights of more than 700 feet. Few realize that this coastline has a grim distinction — that of sharing with King Island, in Bass Strait, and Fraser Island, off the Queensland coast, of being one of Australia's three isles of wrecks. Stormy seas and forbidding reefs and shoals have taken toll of Kangaroo Island's shipping to the extent of 25 major wrecks and an unspecified number of small craft. There are now a number of lighthouses on headlands around the treacherous coast. The interior is hilly and well-wooded, particularly in the west; at Pelican Lagoon (on the east) there is a neck of land only a mile wide.

Pelican Lagoon was so named by Matthew Flinders. He found the islands of this lagoon to be not only a breeding-place for pelicans, 'but from the number of skeletons and bones there scattered, it should seem that they had for ages been selected for the closing scene of their existence'. He rhapsodized over the idea, closing his passage with: 'Alas, for the pelicans! Their golden age is past; but it has much exceeded in duration that of man.' The passage inspired the English poet, James Montgomery, to write his poem, 'Pelican Island'.

It is interesting to note that when Australia was discovered distinct species of emu, smaller than the mainland bird, existed on Kangaroo Island and on King Island in Bass Strait. Both species were exterminated early in the nineteenth century by settlers and sealers, who killed large numbers for food. Of the Kangaroo Island emu (*D. diemenianus*), a single skin and two skeletons are preserved in museums at Paris and Florence. It seems a pity that these relics are housed outside of Australia. The King Island emu (*D. minor*), is known only from bones picked up on the island, and from the brief accounts of one or two early visitors.

It was Matthew Flinders who discovered the island in 1802. Sheltering from a storm while on a voyage of exploration, he later discovered that he had anchored in a protected bay of a large island. The island swarmed with kangaroos that were without fear of man, and Flinders gratefully seized the opportunity to supplement the monotonous and meagre rations for his weary crew. 'In gratitude for so reasonable a supply, I named this southern land Kangaroo Island.'

A few weeks after Flinders departed came the Frenchman, Captain Baudin, and at the township of Penneshaw on the island is a replica of the Frenchman's rock on which is inscribed a permanent record of his visit. The original rock reposes in the Adelaide museum and the inscription, although weather-worn, is still legible. Baudin was responsible for exploring much of the coastline, hence the plethora of bays and capes with French names. The aborigines of the mainland never inhabited Kangaroo Island, but they called it Karta and believed that it had been made by the great god Nurrunduri, a cult-hero of the Narrinyeri tribe whose wives, attempting to swim after him, were turned into the rocky islets now known as The Pages.

Long before the mainland of South Australia was officially settled, there formed on Kangaroo Island a community composed of whalers and convicts escaped from the penal gangs of Tasmania. It must be admitted that the island started off on the wrong foot, for the era was one when lawlessness prevailed and might was right. After the proclamation of South Australia, the island's wild days were numbered and it gradually settled down to an existence of sobriety, albeit remaining an island backwater.

Kangaroo Island is 85 sea miles from Port Adelaide. The drive-on drive-off ferry *Troubridge* provides a six-hour service twice weekly, and there is a daily air service operating from West Beach airport. Despite its old-world atmosphere, Kingscote, the 'capital', with one-third of the island's 2,000 inhabitants, is conscious that it is the hub of the island. It looks squarely at the distant mainland and straggles pleasantly over low rolling hills — a sprinkling of shops and streets, hotels and guest-houses, and a few landmarks with historic background. The inhabitants of the island are mainly engaged in farming, sheep-raising, fishing, and the production of eucalyptus oil. The island is renowned for the latter. From its million-odd acres it is estimated that sufficient eucalyptus oil could be produced to treat all the colds in the world! The yacka gum industry is noteworthy inasmuch that the gum, which is used in the preparation of varnishes and lacquers, comes almost exclusively from the island. Wheat and barley are produced in the rich plains. There is also a thriving tourist trade.

Kingscote and its port are situated on Nepean Bay, 66 feet above sea-level. Nepean Bay was visited in 1802 by Matthew Flinders and also Nicolas Baudin. Within a few years of their visit sealers settled there and it soon became a favourite haunt of sealers, some of whom remained there with Tasmanian aboriginal women as consorts. In July 1836, when the first settlers for the new province of South Australia arrived on the *Duke of York*, islanders brought out a boat-load of vegetables, after making sure that the vessel was not a man-of-war come to discipline their wild life.

Kingscote was the first town site to be decided on in South Australia, and for several months there was talk of

The parade of the Fairy Penguins, Phillip Island, Victoria

Fairy Penguins hatch their young in burrows two or three feet deep

Kangaroo Island, South Australia

More and more tourists are being attracted to the pleasures of island life on Kangaroo Island

making it the capital. For a time it was used as the headquarters of the South Australian Company and the first colonists camped there until the site of Adelaide was chosen. At first Kingscote was named Angas, after one of the pioneers, but, as he objected, it was called Kingscote after Henry Kingscote, a member of the first board of directors of the South Australian Company. In 1838 Kingscote was declared a legal port in order to prevent its becoming (as indeed it was) a smuggling centre.

Kingscote has a venerable mulberry tree more than a century and a quarter old, anchored to the ground by strong iron chains to prevent it being blown down. When Colonel William Light came from England to South Australia in 1836 he had with him a young migrant couple. Only a few days' sail from Kingscote the wife died, and the husband obtained permission from Light to bury his wife on land. On arriving at the spot where Kingscote now stands, the burial service was carried out, the young husband planting a mulberry cutting over the grave.

East of Kingscote is the island's second town, Penneshaw, a quaint little place perched high on cliff tops on the shores of Hog Bay. The latter was so called because at one time large numbers of pigs (introduced from Tasmania) existed on the island. The settlement was first called Hog Bay, but Governor Jervois (1877-83) substituted the present name, compounded, it is said, of the names of his secretary, Penne, and a Miss Shaw. The town overlooks an inviting beach and is close to one of the most picturesque spots on the island, a wide arm of the sea sheltered by low wooded hills and known as American River. In 1803 the crew of an American sealer built a vessel at Pelican Lagoon, the entrance to which was subsequently named American River in commemoration.

The Yankee sealers, or whalers, were thus pioneers in Australian shipbuilding by constructing this, the first, seagoing vessel launched in South Australia. It was a 40-ton schooner named the *Independence* under the supervision of Isaac Pendleton, a visiting sea captain from New York. Incidentally, the same group who launched the *Independence* at American River made the richest haul of sealskins ever collected from South Australian waters when they netted £70,000 from their visit. Considering the value of the pound in those days that sum must have been a vast fortune.

Seals are still plentiful on Kangaroo Island, particularly at Seal Bay, on the south coast of the island. Moreover, they are so tame that they will allow visitors to come right up to them, provided they approach seal-like — on hands and knees. Any attempts to walk to a seal will result in failure. Here in their own environment, the sea and sands, the seals are completely unafraid of bathers and will thoroughly enjoy frolicking with you on the beach. Seal Bay can be reached by road from Kingscote, but the last few miles to the beach are rather rough going. However, exciting rewards are there, cavorting with the seals in the shallows or floundering about in the sand. But remember to approach your aquatic friends on hands and knees.

Kangaroo Island is proud of being the possessor of South Australia's oldest lighthouse and the first which can be said to have been built by a gold rush. The tremendous influx of emigrants to Victoria following the discovery of gold there in 1851, saw many ships passing through the 10-mile-wide Backstairs Passage, which separates south of Adelaide from the island. Because the locality was well studded with dangers for the mariner, the government of the colony decided to erect a light on the granite foundations of Cape Willoughby, the north-eastern point of the island.

Despite its sturdy appearance, the tower was far from waterproof, and pitiful entries by Head Keeper Cawthorne, in the early records, speak of the rain pouring in and the light refusing to burn properly because of the moisture in the air from the still damp whitewash on the walls. There is also an indignant complaint about the crew of a passing brig who landed and stole the store pigs!

Today, more than a century after it was built, the Cape Willoughby lighthouse is still standing as solidly as ever, with three keepers' houses, red and white, nestling around its base. It no longer winks in solitary grandeur, but is answered every six seconds by a flash from the Yatala Shoal buoy, and by the unattended lighthouses on Cape Jervis and Cape St. Albans.

Few can claim to have seen all of Flinders Chase, 210 square miles of Kangaroo Island's virgin scrubland dedicated to the preservation of fauna and flora, embracing almost a third of the island. Many birds and animals from the mainland in danger of extinction have been introduced to this remarkable and ideal habitat for wild life. A number of such fauna and avifauna liberated on the island in 1923 included the rare Cape Barren Geese, Koala Bears, Mallee Hens and Scrub Turkeys. So vast is the area of Flinders Chase that visitors do not always see these birds and animals, but wallabies, kangaroos, emus and opossums, which are in greater numbers, are seen fearlessly roaming through the Chase's dense bush glades. At Rocky River, on the southwest coast, a colony of platypuses was introduced several years ago and appear to be holding their own. Although much of the Chase is easily accessible, so rugged and dense is the growth of the terrain that it still preserves many of its sylvan recesses from all but the most hardy hiker. Apart from its profusion of other native plants, more than 50 species of orchids grow in this reserve.

Flinders Chase has a unique queen-bee breeding station established by the South Australian Government. In 1884 the South Australian Chamber of Commerce imported from Italy a pure strain of Ligurian bee which was distributed to the settlers on Kangaroo Island and where it has been kept pure to the present day. The State's Apiaries Act makes it illegal to introduce any bees whatsoever on to the island. So it is that the golden Ligurians of Flinders Chase in their sanctuary of manna gum, banksia, honeysuckle and other rich native blossoms are regarded as the aristocrats of the bee world. Where breeders on the mainland run the risk of queens mating with undesirable drones from other colonies, this can never happen on Kangaroo Island.

There is nothing streamlined, nothing sophisticated about the island; its very simplicity is its chief delight. Fishing, the tang of the sea, the fascination of watching the white

line of breakers lazily curl on scoured coastline, all fuse
themselves into the island's spell. Standing just outside a
line of wooded hills and looking down the rugged coastline to the lonely cliffs of Cape Borda, with its sentinel
lighthouse, I realized that the virgin beauty of Kangaroo
Island will not always remain thus. Big plans for the developing tourist industry, a stepping-up of greater production and greater settlement are shaking the island out of
its lethargy. To be honest, I find it difficult to report
enthusiastically on this 'progressiveness' that will cause the
island to make up at last for lost time.

23

The Straitsmen

BASS STRAIT, the expanse of ocean lying between the northern coast of Tasmania and the mainland of Australia, is one of this country's great waterways. The strait was discovered by George Bass, the son of Lincolnshire parents who became a village apothecary in his native country before his love for the sea led to his appointment as a naval surgeon. The average width of Bass Strait is about 130 miles with an average depth of about 280 fathoms. Outside the strait the ocean is some 5,000 fathoms deep — conclusive proof, surely, that Tasmania was once part of the mainland.

The biggest islands in the Strait are King, Hunter, Three Hummock and Robbins Island off the north-west tip of Tasmania, and Flinders, Cape Barren and Clarke Island off the north-east tip. Flinders is one of a group of fifty or more islands in the Furneaux group, the group being named for Captain Tobias Furneaux who observed the islands while sailing under Captain Cook. Flinders was named for Matthew Flinders who rescued some of the survivors of the *Sydney Cove* which was wrecked on Preservation Island. Subsequently Flinders engaged in extensive charting of the waters, particularly around Flinders Island.

Flinders Island is approximately 50 miles long and varies in width from eight to 15 miles. From the air it is a quilt-work of farmlets, with some formidable mountain peaks, rugged cliffs and inviting beaches. The highest of the peaks is Mount Strzlecki which rears to 2,700 feet and is the focal point of a very impressive skyline as seen from some distance at sea. Strzlecki and its smaller companions provide some good climbing opportunities to those who follow that recreation or to those who like to get some good island pictures from elevated positions. The rewards offered in the way of scenery from these high spots are rich.

As with the important island of King, the climate on Flinders is mild; there is fishing and game shooting in plenty, and there is a wealth of wildflowers and shrubs, many of them native only to these parts. The islanders raise fat cattle and sheep and the export of wool is considerable. Two other major sources of income are crayfishing and mutton-birding.

Bass Strait was once the haunt of adventurers, desperadoes, gangs of cut-throats and roistering pirates. 'Sea rats and wolves' was how early colonists described these brutal ex-seamen, runaway convicts and other absconders who infested the islands of Bass Strait — given the not inappropriate title of 'Dire Strait' because of its astonishing number of shipwrecks. In many instances vessels were lured to their doom with false lights and signals faked by these sea-roving ruffians. 'A complete set of pirates', wrote the explorer Edmund Lockyer in 1827, and there is no doubt that the islands of the strait were the No-man's-land of these unscrupulous adventurers.

No other part of Australian waters has witnessed such violent scenes of murder, rapine and stark brutality. Escaped convicts and deserters from American sealing vessels and other overseas ships, secure in their storm-lashed and little known island hideouts, cast dreaded shadows over the waters of the strait. Their diabolical operations were generally conducted from the Furneaux Group of islands, and these with the many other islands guarded by dangerous reefs in that area offered them a protection that was almost invulnerable. Cape Barren, Preservation, Goose and innumerable adjacent islands were the scenes of their wild depredations at various times from towards the end of the eighteenth century until well into the last one. Like the traditional pirates they wore gold earrings and kept stocks of kegged rum salvaged from wrecks, or looted in raids on the high seas, but their clothing was often made from kangaroo-skin with caps fashioned from seal-skins.

Before the Bass Strait islands were taken over by the desperadoes, the waters of this area were Australia's first great sealing venture. In October 1798 Captain Charles Bishop and his crew of the 56-ton brig *Nautilus* collected 9,000 skins at Cape Barren Island. The following year the schooner *Martha* entered Sydney Harbour with 1,300 seal-skins obtained in Bass Strait. Whaling attained such heavy proportions that within a few years the supply of seals in Bass Strait was seriously depleted. The Australian Sea Bear, once numerous in the islands, is now rarely seen. The great Sea Elephant, which derives its name from its long snout, also deserted Bass Strait where it abounded, the ruthless destruction by the early hunters being again responsible.

With the professional full-time sealers leaving Bass Strait for other grounds, the islands were left to the 'Straitsmen' where far from the restraints of authority the men lived by their own brutal code. Periodically they would descend upon the Tasmanian coast and raid the aboriginal camps for young women, and it mattered not if the gins had infants at the breast, for, heedless of the piteous cries of the mothers they would snatch the babies and dash out their brains. 'These women,' wrote a contemporary historian in a report he furnished to the Colonial Secretary in 1815, 'are kept as slaves, hunting and foraging for the sealers who transfer and dispose of them one to the other as their own property. Very few ever see their native homes or families again. If they do not comply with orders in hunting and sealing, their white masters, by way of punishment, half hang them, cut their heads with clubs in a shocking manner or flog them unmercifully with "cats" made of kangaroo sinews.'

These outrages on Tasmanian aboriginal women did more than anything else to aggravate native hostility toward white settlers. Thrashed if they did not work hard enough skinning the seals or cleaning mutton-birds, these women were expert at seal catching; swimming underwater among a herd of seals, their black skin resembling their quarry, they would club or knife the animals to death. There are now no aborigines on these islands nor even in Tasmania itself; the last of them died in the sanctuary set aside for them on Flinders Island.

In 1839 the brig *Brittomart* carrying a number of passengers and a full cargo sailed from Melbourne for Tasmania, but neither the ship nor those on board was ever seen again. When she was listed as considerably overdue, the Government schooner *Sir John Franklin* was sent in search and a call was made at some of the Bass Strait islands. It was found that inhabitants of Preservation Island were bedecked in good clothes and jewellery but, although a snuff-box bearing the initials of one of the missing passengers was picked up on the beach by the *Franklin's* master, they denied all knowledge of the lost ship or those aboard her. Newspaper reports of that time were of the opinion that the vessel had been lured on to Goose Island by false lights, scuttled, and her people murdered. Today on Preservation Island can be seen relics of the dwelling of James Monro who was known as the 'King of the Eastern Straitsmen'. Monro, a notorious character, lived there for more than thirty years and had a retinue of black wives.

Preservation Island was the scene of the wreck of the *Sydney Cove* — the first recorded wreck in Tasmanian waters. On a grey morning in February 1797, the vessel, running before a gale, slid slowly onto a sandbank in 19 feet of water within sight of Preservation Island in the Furneaux Group. As yet unnamed, that small isle to the west of Cape Barren Island was given the name 'Preservation'. When the ship's company was safely landed, a well was dug in the sand and provided drinkable water, the first essential to survival.

From their place of safety the castaways could see the wreck, wallowing and swaying under the hammers of the ocean, but held by the sand from sinking further. Captain Hamilton, seeing his ship lost and his men saved, took stock of the position. He was on the uncharted southern seas of Australia; the little settlement at Port Jackson was less than ten years old; there was scarcely a chance of rescue

190

as George Bass had only just discovered the existence of
Bass Strait, and shipping was wide of the scene of shipwreck. Help would have to be sought, so the first sixteen
days the marooned men spent in equipping a lifeboat. When
the frail craft was finished seventeen men took their places
in her to set sail for Port Jackson. The men remaining
on the island were safe, and when they had farewelled the
lifeboat settled down into the existence of so many Robinson Crusoes. After an appalling journey the lifeboat was
wrecked on the Ninety Mile Beach of Gippsland and the
men began a several hundred miles walk to Botany Bay.
When two months later three of them reached Sydney
they told of how exhaustion, exposure, hunger and hard-
ship had claimed the other fourteen. However, there was
no delay in setting out for the rescue of the marooned
sailors on Preservation Island. Governor Hunter sent the
10-ton sloop *Francis* to the wreck to bring off the remainder
of the crew and some of the cargo.

Just as James Monro was the self-styled 'King of the
Eastern Straitsmen', so David Howie who lived on Robbins
Island was the acknowledged leader of the Western Straits-
men. Howie was there until as late as 1854, and when the
emigrant ship *Cataraqui* was wrecked on King Island in
August 1845 he buried more than 300 victims.

Captain William Smith of the brig *Caledonia* was one of
several shady mariners who traded with the straitsmen,
exchanging barrels of rum for seal-skins and various ships'
cargo. No questions were asked as to how the latter was
obtained. Smith knew the dark, treacherous waters of Bass
Strait as few other navigators did, and all his dealings were
carried out in the lonely anchorages of the strait. On one
occasion in 1828 he took the *Caledonia* to a secluded shore
on Preservation Island and began a mysterious transforma-
tion. The *Caledonia* was altered from a brig to a schooner,
painted and decorated entirely different. Equally mysteriously, strange men — mostly escaped convicts — began to
arrive on the island by whale-boat and join the schooner-
brig's crew.

Whether Captain Smith meditated a buccaneering expedition with this hard-bitten crew or whether he had merely contracted to carry escaped convicts out of the country will never be known. H.M.S. *Duke of York* sailed into the anchorage — someone must have tipped-off the authorities — and arrested the *Caledonia*. The *Duke of York* ran aground on Maria Island and three of the prisoners escaped in one of the naval ship's boats, but eventually the *Caledonia* was escorted back to Hobart. The resourceful Smith, however, assumed an air of righteous innocence, and although the authorities had very strong suspicions about the captain's intentions nothing could be proved and he was freed. Smith took the *Caledonia* to the Philippines where his shady activities resulted in a clash with the Spanish Governor-General at Manila who ordered him out of Philippine territory. He returned to the more profitable waters of Bass Strait which he knew so well.

The last known act of piracy by the straitsmen was in 1852 when the schooner *Mary* was forcibly taken and run ashore at Clarke Island. Her Majesty's brig-of-war *Fantome* was one of the vessels patrolling these waters with cannon loaded and men ready for action, ever ready to intercept escaping convicts in longboats or overtake ships of doubtful ownership. But the law-breakers frequently eluded the net.

The Bass Strait islanders of today — descendants of the straitsmen and their native wives — are sound and honest. Indeed, they are models of law-abiding people; prosperous farms and enterprises have replaced the hut shanties and caves where the outlaws of the Strait once lived.

24

Metropolitan Islands

FOR THOSE who like island life close to civilization, or even near a metropolis, their wishes can be satisfied, All the Australian coastal cities have nearby islands, some of them so close they can only be regarded as suburbs. Those in Port Jackson are largely ignored by Sydneysiders, many of whom would find difficulty in naming the nine islands of their harbour. In part they are ignored because the people of Sydney have so little contact with them; yet an island such as Goat, which is no more than a mile from the Sydney G.P.O., would be many people's idea of paradise.

Goat Island has everything — except goats. And as far as historians can tell, there never was so much as a solitary nanny on it. All they know is that the aborigines called it Mel Mel — 'Eye of the Harbour' — and that some years before Governor Bourke began a penal settlement there in 1833 a long-forgotten humorist called it Goat Island. Maybe he was one of the convicts who later built the great stone wall, the arsenal with its six-foot-thick walls, and the barracks there. However, the island boasts 14 sheep who live a life of luxury — and act as mobile lawnmowers at the same time. There can be few sheep who live their soft city life with nothing to do all day but eat grass that never dries up. And for a change of diet the island children hand-feed them stale bread.

The whole life of the island is linked with the sea, and all around its shores are ideal fishing spots where the inhabitants can settle down for a quiet hour without fear of competition. The children are shipped to and from school by special launch. Even the housewives have to go to the mainland because Goat Island hasn't a single shop. Anyhow, shops are surely out of place on a small island. Nor is there a post office, school, or movie show. The islanders are so close to the city there is no need for any. It takes only 12 minutes by ferry to reach Circular Quay, yet the island, in many ways, is out of Sydney's world. People talk of 'going ashore' or 'staying on board' when it's a question of going to Sydney or not, and they refer to the island as 'she'. Mail deliveries and essentials such as bread, meat and milk arrive by regular service in a special Maritime launch. The milkman's launch comes every morning about six-thirty. But whenever an islander wants to leave for the shore he has to hoist high the signal flag so a passing ferry will call.

The island is the headquarters of Sydney's water fire brigade. There are two shifts, each of 16 firemen, who, with their families are permanent residents. About 150 others come to work at the island daily, at the headquarters of the Maritime Services Board, which has shipbuilding and repair yards there.

Highly interesting are the original buildings on the island with their high walls, imposing gates and sentry boxes. A most impressive structure is the magazine, 100 feet long and 35 feet wide, with walls six feet thick surmounted by an arched roof. Other military buildings include the homes of the officers and the guard house erected in white sandstone quarried on the island. On the walls of stone sentry boxes soldiers have cut their names.

Another relic is the convict's 'chair', cut into a rock. This was the home of Charles Anderson, transported to New South Wales when he was eighteen years old. Because of his several attempts at escape he was chained to the rock for two years with barely a rag to cover him. He was fastened by his waist to the rock with a chain twenty-six feet long and with trumpet irons on his legs. A hollow, scooped out in the large rock big enough to admit his body, served for his bed, and his only shelter was a wooden lid perforated with holes, which was placed over him and locked in that position at night, being removed in the morning. He was fed by means of a pole with which the vessel containing his food was pushed towards him. None of his fellow prisoners were permitted to approach or speak to him under a penalty of a hundred lashes. Regarded as a wild beast, people passing in boats would throw him bits of bread or biscuit.

The juxtaposition of past and present on Goat Island is as striking as the isolation of its small community, so near and yet so far from sprawling Sydney.

Clarke Island, a recreation reserve beautifully maintained by the Sydney Harbour Trust, is well worth a visit. It was named after a marine who served in the 'First Fleet' and is principally used in the summer time as a splendid vantage point from which to view the sailing races, which start and finish near there. Opposite Rose Bay is Shark Island, formerly a quarantine ground for animals, now a recreation reserve maintained by the Government, and also a favourite spot from which to watch the sailing races. On these and other islands in Sydney Harbour may be found much hidden beauty, relics of early colony days, and superb sights for watching the great shipping traffic of Port Jackson whose area covers no less than 22 square miles with a coastline of approximately 200 miles.

Peers and poets have proclaimed the glories of Port Jackson. Lord Rosebery, Prime Minister of Britain in the middle nineties of last century, summed it up in a matchless phrase, 'Where gates of granite give entrance to a paradise of waters.' Henry Lawson, toiling out beyond Coolgardie at the time Lord Rosebery wrote, was nostalgic for Sydney and its harbour when he penned the lines:

'Oh, there never dawned a morning in the long and lonely days,
But I thought I saw the ferries steaming out across the bays,
And as fresh and fair in fancy did the picture rise again
As the sunrise flushed the city from Woollahra to Balmain.

'And the sunny water frothing round the liners, black and red,

And the coastal steamers working by the loom of Bradley's Head;
And the whistles and the sirens that re-echo far and wide —
All the life and light and beauty that belong to Sydney-side.

'And the dreary cloud-line never veiled the end of one day more,
But the City, set in jewels, rose before me from "The Shore".
Round the sea-world shine the beacons of a thousand ports o'
    call,
But the harbour lights of Sydney are the grandest of them all.'

Three islands off the Australian coast are named Phillip.
One lies near Norfolk Island, another off the north-eastern
shore of Macquarie Harbour, Tasmania, and the third and
largest at the entrance to Westernport in south-central Victoria. The latter island is a popular tourist resort within
easy travelling distance of Melbourne and elsewhere in
southern Victoria. About 13 miles long and 8 miles wide,
its area of some 60 square miles has many scenic attractions.
The southern coastline is composed of rocky headlands
interspersed with good surfing beaches, and tourists are well
served with fishing, boating and swimming facilities. A
never-ending source of interest are the koala reserves and
the colonies of seals, mutton-birds and fairy penguins.

Phillip Island was discovered in 1798 by George Bass who
described its highest point, Cape Woolamai (358 feet) as
'a high cape, like a snapper's head'. James Grant of H.M.S.
Lady Nelson made a similar comment, and hence came its
first name, Snapper Island. Later it was known as Grant
Island — the western extremity is called Grant Point — but
eventually the name Phillip Island (in honour of Governor
Phillip) became established. An interesting fact is that the
first plantings to be sown in Victoria were made at Phillip
Island. James Grant in 1801 planted there wheat, various
vegetables, and seeds of apples, plums and peaches, 'together
with a few grains of rice and coffee'. Nearly 40 years later
the island was occupied by two Scottish brothers, William
and John McHaffie, as a station property. They ran flocks
of sheep and raised pedigreed cattle and horses, one of
which, Wollamai, won several races. In the 1860s The Ac-
climatization Society of Victoria carried out successful ex-

periments in the breeding of game-birds — quail, pheasants, partridge and such like — on the island.

Most tourists make their headquarters on the sheltered northern shore where the main settlements — Cowes, Ventnor, Rhyll and Newhaven are located. A bridge connects Newhaven to the mainland at San Remo and there is also a ferry service between Cowes and Stony Point to the northwest.

Hundreds of penguins and seals dwell in their native state on that part of Phillip Island known as The Nobbies, and it is there that the summer attraction for tourists is the nightly parade of the fairy penguins. For as long as Victorians can remember, these tiny marine birds (from eight to ten inches high) have been putting on a performance as quaint and delightful as you could wish to see. It lasts for half or three quarters of an hour and holds the audience spellbound. It begins each evening with a sudden yapping puppy-like noise heard above the pounding of the surf on the beach. The audience, warmly clad in slacks, overcoats and sweaters, the children in dressing gowns over their pyjamas, ready for bed, rises excitedly from outspread rugs and peers intently at the rolling breakers. Suddenly a spotlight on the beach picks out a lonely little blue-grey figure with a white front which gleams in the strong beam, swimming shorewards. He is buffeted and swept out of sight by the curling foam, but soon more and more of his kind appear among the breakers making slow but certain progress to the beach.

Once on land the fairy penguins flap their wings vigorously and with ceaseless chatter await the rest of their fellows. Then to the squeals of delight from young and old in the audience the parade of the fairy penguins begins. Oblivious of the watching audience or the blinding glare from the spotlights played on them, nothing seems to perturb the quaint little creatures as they march in orderly procession across the white sands and up the steep sandhills to their burrows. In the half-light of evening the dapper little forms suggest small-scale human figures in dress clothes. On arriving at the rookeries they settle themselves for the night,

197

but seemingly with never a thought of sleep. Their chattering continues unendingly and one can imagine them gossiping about their daily doings, the size of the fish they caught, and the long day's swim.

The fairy penguins adhere to a strict regular family-life routine. Husband and wife take turns each day sitting on the eggs, while the other swims all day for food — up to 70 miles daily — and returns at dusk with sufficient fish for supper and breakfast. Even when the chicks are hatched, one 'baby-sits' while the other goes off to gather the fish supply. For the first three months of their lives the chicks are 'under the flippers' of their parents. Round little balls of fur, they play in and about their cosy burrows peeking curiously at the outside world, but never venturing more than a few feet away. At the end of this period their parents leave them for good to fend for themselves. The bewildered babies live off the fat of their own bodies for a week or more and then, hunger overriding their timidity, cautiously make their way to the water's edge, take their first plunge — and swim for their own suppers.

The fairy penguin is the only species (there are about 17 members of the penguin group in the world) resident in Australian seas. It extends as far north as the New South Wales-Queensland border on the east and the Houtman Abrolhos on the west. In most instances the nests are placed on islands — two white eggs are laid in springtime — but occasionally a colony adopts a spot on the mainland.

The estimated fairy penguin population of Phillip Island is about 4,000. The Cowes Shire, in which the island is incorporated, sees that the birds are protected, and there are always members of a special protection committee on duty there. They have erected a strong wire fence around the 'parade-ground' to keep people from making too close contact with these tiny penguins so as not to disturb their age-long routine.

Through the heart of the capital city of Queensland wind the broad waters of the Brisbane River to greet the vast expanse of island-studded Moreton Bay. As the city drops behind near the end of the river's 214-miles journey, pelican, wild duck and swan abound until at last is reached the almost land-locked bay. Here in these 735 square miles of sparkling waters are groups and clusters of islands far removed from the hurly-burly and breathless activity of city life, yet within a short distance of the Queensland capital.

Some of these islands are large and well clothed with timber and vegetation, with a shoreline of gently shelving sandy beaches and rocky forelands; some are flat and sandy, sparsely covered with low scrub and coarse grasses, while others are barely above high water mark and fringed with extensive mangrove trees growing to the water's edge. On several islands in Canaipa Passage, in the south of the bay, agriculture is flourishing and farms are producing large quantities and varieties of tropical fruit.

Leading through these thronging islands are winding channels and passages, some navigable only by very small craft, and others deep and wide enough for sizeable yachts and launches to thread their way through the intricate maze of islands and sandbanks. Cruising and fishing in the bay are very popular and every week-end and holiday see scores of sailing boats, launches and yachts making their way to Pumicestone Passage in the north, with the Glass House Mountains on the mainland silhouetted sharply against the sky. And to Comboyura, Cowan Cowan and the former whaling station at Tangalooma on Moreton Island — to the reefs at Peel Island and the coves and inlets at Jumpin Pin in the south, and to many another favoured spot in this bay of islands.

The largest of the islands — Bribie, Moreton and Stradbroke — protect the inner waterlanes from the ceaseless roll of the Pacific. Stradbroke and Moreton were named by Captain Cook when he passed by in 1770. Nine years later Matthew Flinders explored Moreton Bay and its labyrinth of islands, but the entrance to the Brisbane River remained a well-hidden secret until 1823 when Pamphlett, Finigan and Parsons, three ticket-of-leave convicts, were wrecked on the shores of Moreton Island. In that same year they told of the great river to explorer John Oxley, who took two whaleboats upstream in search of a new convict settlement.

Hundreds of small islands cluster at the southern end of Moreton Bay and it is a delight to cruise among them on a typical blue and gold day. On leaving the river and entering the bay you pass the Fisherman Islands, a group numbering thirty small isles. Then Green Island and St. Helena, a penal settlement until as late as 1931, slip by. Rich red volcanic soil is found on the islands of Coochi, Mudlo, Garden, Karra Garra and Macley, all of which grow tropical fruits. It is a delightful surprise to go ashore at one of these fertile islands amid a grove of tall banana trees, or row upon row of pineapples, their fruit growing golden amongst the spiny leaves. Then there are paw paws hanging in clusters beneath their umbrella-like foliage. Russel Island has 120 of such thriving tropical fruit farms in this idyllic setting of placid waters.

There is more than beauty around the islands of the great bay. The winding channels and passages are pathways of the sea which once guided early explorers, and they abound with stories of historical interest and rollicking tales of adventure. There is drama behind many of the wrecks on Bishop Island, near the river's mouth. Among those hulks are the *Lochiel* and *Roderick Dhu,* once engaged in 'blackbirding' — the bringing of kanakas from islands in the Pacific to work in the canefields of North Queensland. On Bishop Island also are the remains of the *Bingera,* a record-holding mail steamer of her day, plying between Brisbane and North Queensland before the days of railways. History was made on the decks of the *Lucinda* when State Premiers met to draw up the draft of the Constitution of Australia prior to Federation.

Tall pines and an olive grove on St. Helena, and the old prison buildings are reminders that this fertile volcanic island was a penal settlement where prisoners also raised prize cattle which played an important part in improving the blood stock of the State.

The Moreton Bay islands are rich, too, in aboriginal legend — and native names give picturesque meaning to those which have been retained. Jumpin Pin means 'place of big waves', and to the natives Stradbroke Island was known as Dumba, meaning 'land of lakes'. The Blue Lake on Stradbroke was called Karboora — 'the dreaded place' — where native chiefs were buried by setting them adrift on a blazing raft.

Moreton Island was known to the aborigines as Moolginpin, which means 'where hills reach the sun'. According to their legends, Moolginpin and Dumba were once joined. Mirripool, the Wind Caller, inherited a shell to control the winds. The Nooghies of Moolginpin stole it, rousing the wrath of Mirripool, who called on the Four Winds to destroy the land-link between Moolginpin and Dumba. This break was named Shagoo — 'talking waters' — because natives could speak across the narrow passage, now known as the South Passage.

Stradbroke Island is thirty-seven miles long and ten miles wide. Rich in bird life, and with a profusion of interesting plants, it has three settlements — Amity Point, Dunwich and Point Lookout. The scenery at Point Lookout is dramatic and beautiful with bold forelands, sheltered inlets, grassy slopes and miles of unbroken surfing beaches. At the base of Point Lookout, separated by a deep channel, is Whale Rock and its eerie blowhole. Alongside the point is a rocky gorge with steep grassy slopes falling away to the lip of the bare cliff walls. Into this chasm race mountainous waves to crash on the rocks and send huge clouds of spray leaping high into the air.

Close by this magnificent spectacle is the Bathing Gorge, a pandanus adorned inlet ideal for all-year-round swimming. The headlands protect the fine sandy beach with its strong-running surf from boisterous winds and it is perfect for lazy sunbathing or vigorous surfing. On either side of Point Lookout extend long stretches of splendid beaches, and pleasant walks may be made to several lagoons, secluded fern gullies and the beautiful Blue Lake. In their graphic language, the aborigines had named Point Lookout 'Mooloomba', meaning 'Rocks warmed by the sun', and from the rocks and craggy headlands keen anglers get fine hauls. Black bass frequent the narrow gorges, and jewfish and sweetlip are plentiful. Many a good catch, too, is made from the surf.

Amity Point, on Stradbroke Island, is approached through Rous Channel, or the alternative route via the colourful Rainbow Passage. Amity takes its name from the brig *Amity* which landed thrice-convicted felons in 1824. They were marched along the island to the present site of Dunwich. In early colonial days Amity was then a signal station, and at the turn of the century yachtsmen gathered there to picnic and conduct sporting events at the racecourse, long since overgrown. Amity Point has a pretty bushland setting with quiet swimming beaches, especially favoured by fishermen during the whiting and bream season.

Tranquil, too, are the surroundings of Dunwich. But the atmosphere was not always so, and echoes of the grim past whisper across the bay from the days when it began its history as a penal settlement. Dunwich became in turn a Quarantine Station and a Government Benevolent Institution for the aged until 1946. From its heights a spectacular panorama of Moreton Bay spreads as far as the eye can see, with the islands of Peel, Bird and Goat in the foreground. Today there is an aboriginal settlement at Myora, a few miles from Dunwich, centre of oyster farming. Roads and tracks lead to the many lakes, lagoons and beaches of Stradbroke, and to the mines where minerals are being extracted from the beach sands in large quantities.

Since 1950 mineral treatment works have been established on the site of the old Benevolent Home at Dunwich producing rutile, zircon and monazite. Suction dredges work on sand dunes on the ocean side of the island producing concentrates which are delivered to Dunwich by the longest aerial ropeway in Queensland — a distance of seven miles — always a source of interest to visitors.

The dazzling white shores of Stradbroke Island are remarkably rich in beach-sand, particularly zircon, rutile, monazite and ilmenite. All of these minerals have a high specific gravity and are chemically stable and resistant to disintegration. Incidentally, Australia's beaches, mostly in

North Queensland, are the world's main source of supply of rutile and zircon.

There is a rustic charm about Bribie Island with its cool green valleys and forested hills. Long and narrow, it has an area of 59 square miles from Toorbul Point to Caloundra, with the blue Pacific on one side and the smooth waters of Deception Bay and Pumicestone Passage on the other. On the channel side is the township of Bongaree and a settlement at Ocean Beach bearing another aboriginal name — Woorim. Here on the ocean side is a glorious surfing beach stretching for almost twenty-five miles. Between Bongaree and Woorim is a connecting road flanked by tall trees and open bushland. The island is a sanctuary for all wild life, and it is not unusual to see kangaroos, wallabies and other animals, together with prolific bird life in their native state. The unspoiled natural beauty of Bribie entices the visitor to explore its many bush tracks, lagoons, inviting beaches with views over Pumicestone Passage to the Glass House Mountains, or inland to forest groves and glades.

From the vantage point of towering headlands on the ocean side of any of these main islands are magnificent seascapes of stretches of glistening sand extending into the hazy distance, and the restless surf crashing on the beach in misty clouds of fine spray. Out to sea are isolated rocks and reefs, momentarily lost to view as waves surge over them, and sometimes may be seen the exciting display of whales at play or huge schools of mullet moving northward along the coast.

Inland is the quiet hush of the bushland where one may wander at will through the shady valleys and over the forested slopes of these peaceful regions. Caught in the spell of the islands, we identify ourselves, our minds, with the grandeur and beauty, the solace and serenity of ageless things.

I would wash the dust of the world in a soft green flood:
Here, between sea and sea, in the fairy wood,
I have found a delicate, wave-green solitude . . .

Index

209

211

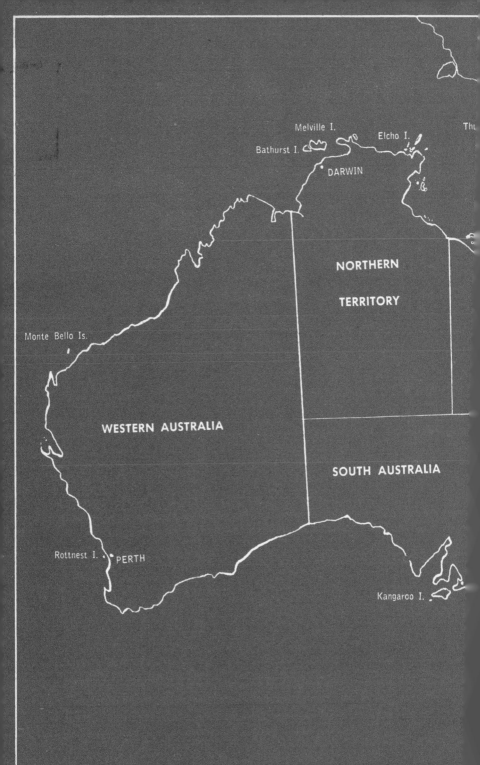